Calhoun School
433 West End
New York N

The French Foreign Legion

Under the scorching rays of the Sahara sun, the legionnaires in their white kepis plodded wearily along. They seemed to be fighting two great enemies at once – the murderous Berber tribesmen, and the cruel barren desert.

In these pages, the author tells the stirring story of the French Foreign Legion from its foundation in 1830 to the present day. He paints a vivid picture of what life was like for the ordinary soldier in this strange independent army – the boredom and long hours of back-breaking training, the harsh treatment by sadistic sergeants, the agonies of malaria and desert madness, the ferocious skirmishes with merciless Arabs, the constant fear of torture and death. And we see how the rogues and runaways, misfits and murderers who made up the French Foreign Legion were moulded into one of the finest fighting forces the world has ever known.

NIGEL THOMAS studied French and German at the University of Manchester. After some years working in Europe, he now teaches at a large comprehensive school in Sunderland. His interests include military uniforms, history, and travel.

A WAYLAND SENTINEL BOOK

The French Foreign Legion

Nigel Thomas

Legio Patria Nostra
The Legion is our Homeland
Motto of the French Foreign Legion.

More Sentinel Books

Frontispiece: The Foreign Legion in Morocco – two
Chinese legionnaires read a letter from home, May 1931.

ISBN 85340 197 7

Copyright © 1973 by Wayland Publishers Ltd
49 Lansdowne Place, Hove, Sussex BN3 1HF
2nd Impression 1980
Set in 'Monophoto' Baskerville and
printed offset litho in Great Britain by
Page Bros (Norwich) Ltd, Norwich

Contents

List of Illustrations

1. The Legion is born

The 1830 revolution in France brought a new king, Louis-Philippe, to the throne. Louis-Philippe was already in his fifties. A man with a small beard and moustache, and dark flashing eyes, he had few friends. Now, as King, he was suspicious of everyone, and lived in constant fear of attempts to overthrow him.

For hundreds of years, soldiers from Switzerland, Ireland, Germany and other nations had served in the French army. Louis-Philippe was afraid that because these soldiers weren't French, they would feel no loyalty towards him. So one of his first acts as King was to disband these foreign regiments.

The soldiers, about two thousand of them, were paid, then locked out of the barracks where they lived and told to go home to their own country. Many of them could not speak French, but they did not return home. Instead, they spent their pay on drink. Then they began to steal money from people in the street, and soon the police were receiving many angry complaints. The King realized that these foreigners were now more dangerous than ever. There was only one thing to do. They must be tricked into leaving France.

So, on 9th March, 1831, Louis-Philippe announced: "A special legion will be formed for foreigners, to be called the *Légion Etrangère* (Foreign Legion). No Frenchman will be allowed to enlist in it."

Louis-Philippe was sure that these hungry, penniless, ex-soldiers would be glad to join the army again. Once the Legion was formed he could send it far from France, away to the deserts of North Africa, where the French army was locked in conflict with the Algerians.

Opposite Louis-Philippe became King of France in 1830. His fear of foreign mercenaries in the French army led him to form the French Foreign Legion, in the hope of getting rid of them.

The men of the Legion

The first commander of the French Foreign Legion was a very experienced Swiss soldier, Colonel Stoffel – a small man with bushy black eyebrows and a single-minded determination to succeed. He had served loyally and bravely in the old Hohenlohe Legion for most of his life, but he still spoke French with a thick Swiss-German accent.

Stoffel was allowed to accept only foreigners as soldiers. But he could recruit some French officers and sergeants to help him. It was largely through

Above The men of the Foreign Legion were recruited from among the thugs and adventurers of Europe, and soon earned the reputation of being even more tough and hard-drinking than most soldiers.

bribery that he managed to do so. Yet, with their help, he managed to turn a mixed bunch of misfits into one of the finest units in the French army.

The ordinary soldiers who volunteered to serve Stoffel came from a dozen different countries in Europe, and joined for a hundred different reasons. There were tough, arrogant Polish soldiers who had fled from Poland after its conquest by Russian forces. There were Spaniards and Italians who proved to be extremely brave fighters, especially when a battle was going against them. They were joined by Swiss and Germans – solid, hard-working peasants, who would follow an officer they respected into any danger. There were also a few Belgians and Dutch, as well as some Russians and Hungarians. But no Englishmen or Americans joined the Legion until about 1870.

Many Frenchmen were admitted illegally. Some of them were criminals whom the French authorities wanted to be rid of. Others were simply escaping from lives of drudgery and hardship. They, and many Frenchmen after them, pretended to be French-speaking Swiss or Belgians, and enlisted in the Legion under a false name.

Although the official recruiting age was between eighteen and forty, many boys of fifteen and sixteen, and some old men of sixty managed to lie their way into the Legion. The gruff Colonel Stoffel would accept anyone who wanted to join badly enough. Some people joined to find a life of adventure. Others hoped to find a new life, to grow rich in the unknown land of Algeria. There were tramps and drunkards, and greedy mercenary soldiers. They were all men that France did not want, and was happy to get rid of.

Legion organization

In the summer of 1831, Colonel Stoffel began to gather his men in Paris. The haughty French High Command insisted that the Legion should be organized as quickly as possible. King Louis-Philippe wanted this noisy rabble off the streets of Paris, and off the soil of France, immediately. This impatience annoyed Stoffel but, characteristically, he carried on without complaining.

Within four weeks just over three thousand men, enough to form a large regiment, had reported to the Paris recruiting office. There the French officer asked each man a few simple questions in French. But often the foreigners could not understand him, and confusion arose.

"Your name?" the officer would snap.

"I am Polish, Monsieur," a man might reply.

It was not going to be easy for Stoffel to command a regiment made up of so many different nationalities. The men were often unable to understand any language other than their own. This decided Stoffel to divide the Legion into seven different battalions, with each battalion consisting of men of the same

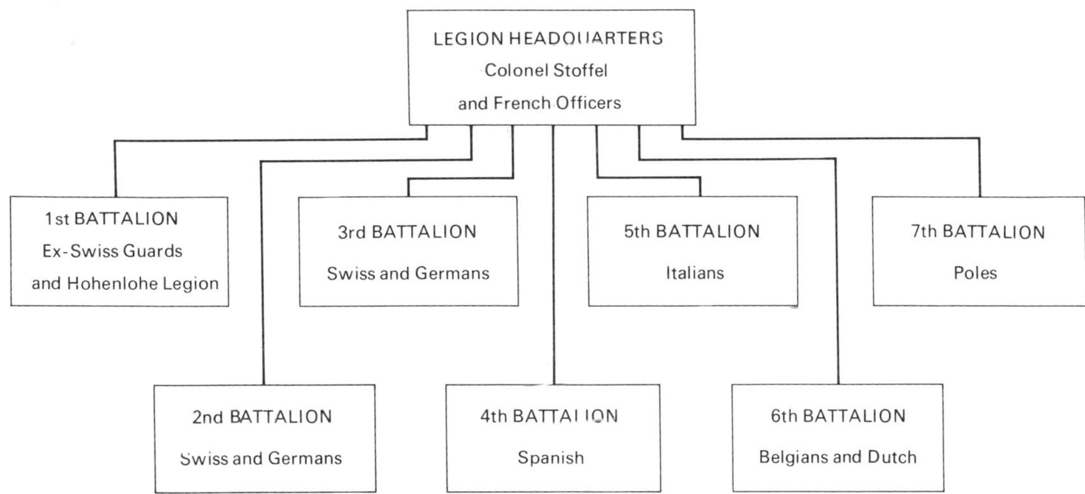

nationality. In this way the men would at least understand each other, and be happy to work together; and the French officers and sergeants were then encouraged to learn the language of the men they commanded.

Because of this national grouping, the size of the battalions varied. The Second and Third Battalions, composed of Swiss and Germans, had more than seven hundred men each, whilst the Spanish Fourth Battalion had only three hundred and fifty.

Yet, despite Stoffel's careful precautions, trouble broke out. The Polish recruits picked fights with the Germans, and the Spaniards often got drunk and attacked any officer who came near them. The people of Paris had hoped that such violence would stop when the Legion was formed. Stoffel did his best to control his men, but he knew that news of the fights would soon reach the High Command.

As usual he was right. In September, 1831, the Legion was ordered to leave France at once for Algeria.

First Algerian conflict

The first part of the journey to Africa was by train to Marseilles. The long-suffering citizens of Paris heaved a sigh of relief as the train carrying the Legion pulled slowly out from the station. The officers sat in second-class carriages and the ordinary soldiers were crammed together in dirty, smelly, cattle-trucks behind.

The voyage across the blue calm of the Mediterrean Sea lasted four days, and there was wild excitement when the bustling port of Algiers, with its low white houses and tall thin minarets, at last came into sight.

The weary soldiers, though, were surprised and hurt when the ship's captain just dumped them on the quayside – the French authorities had not been warned of their arrival. Colonel Stoffel was furious. He bullied the local garrison commander until beds, food and rifles were provided for him and his men. Eventually uniforms arrived , too, but these consisted of heavy blue coats and bright red trousers meant for the cold French winters and not the sweltering Algerian sun.

Gradually the size of the Legion grew. By March, 1832, Stoffel had five thousand men under his command. But when orders at last came through

Left This was the first glimpse of Algiers for many of the new recruits.

Top right The French North African colony of Algeria, scene of the Legion's early fame.

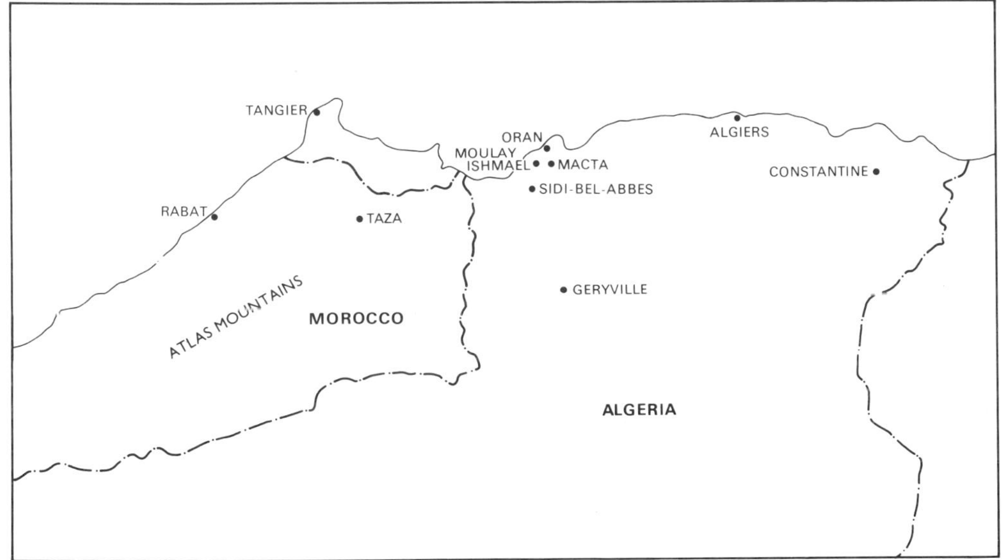

from the High Command in France, his troops were told to build a road from Algeria eastward along the coast. Stoffel was livid that the army should treat his unit with such contempt.

But the chance of a fight soon came. Abd-el-Kader, a wily Algerian sheikh, rose in revolt against the hated French under old General Guizot. All available forces were brought up to fight the rebels, including the Legion.

No one expected the legionnaires to distinguish themselves, but they proved to be the best soldiers the French had. In July, 1835, they fought at the Battle of Moulay Ishmael, when the French were forced to retreat. The Battle of Macta, a month later, was another diaster and the victorious Abd-el-Kader drove the weary French back towards Oran. Indeed, the Arabs would have captured Oran but for the sturdy Poles of the Seventh Battalion, who delayed the rebel forces long enough to let the main French column organize a successful defence of the city.

Disaster in Spain

The defeats of Moulay Ishmael and Macta left General Guizot in disgrace. He had to admit: "Those thieves and drunkards of a Foreign Legion fought magnificently."

Colonel Stoffel had been replaced in March, 1834, by Colonel Claude Bernelle, a strong and handsome French infantry officer. In August, 1835, Bernelle led the battered but triumphant Legion back to the base-camp in Algiers, and promised that the

legionnaires would have a few days of complete rest. His rage was all the greater, then, when he read the orders there waiting for him. He was told to leave for Spain at once. The bravery the Legion had shown at Moulay Ishmael only served to make it more unpopular with the High Command.

In November, 1834, a Civil War had broken out in Spain. The Royalist or Christino army, led by the Queen Regent, Isobel, was fighting rebel forces, the Carlists, for control of the Spanish throne. Isobel appealed to King Louis-Philippe of France for help. The latter was reluctant to send any French troops to die in a war that could in no way benefit France. But then he remembered the Legion, and his fears of those wild foreigners. Spain seemed a good place to send them to die.

In September, 1835, the Legion landed at Tarragona in Spain, and stayed there for three harsh years. At the Battle of Aragona in March, 1837, they were almost completely massacred in a pitched battle against a huge Carlist army. Most of the legionnaires who died in Spain, however, were not killed by bullets. The corrupt Christino army often refused to pay, feed or shelter the men. The Spanish General Catanez kept the money sent from France for himself, and the legionnaires died of malaria or frostbite during the bitterly cold winters.

And still the Civil War dragged on. By December, 1838, five hundred legionnaires were left out of the five thousand who had landed at Tarragona. But a crueller blow was yet to come. The French High Command suddenly announced that the brave men who had suffered so badly in a war they did not even understand, were to be abandoned. The Legion was too small. It must be disbanded, and the men left to make their own way home.

2. The desert war

In Algeria, General Guizot had been happy to see the Legion leave for Spain. But, as Abd-el-Kader's army grew in size, and his tribesmen won more victories, Guizot began to panic. He now regretted losing the brave foreigners who had fought so well for France, and whom she had treated so badly. He asked the High Command to order the Legion back to Algeria. But his request was turned down.

In December, 1835, Guizot wrote to Louis-Philippe himself, asking permission to form a second

Foreign Legion. At first Louis-Philippe refused. Then Guizot sent him a telegram with these few ominous words: "Without the Legion you will lose Algeria."

Louis-Philippe was convinced. On 20th December, 1835, he proclaimed that recruiting for a new Foreign Legion would begin at once.

Throughout 1836, men from all over Europe signed on to join the new Legion. But the numbers grew very slowly. By January, 1837, there were no more than eight hundred recruits, enough only for one battalion. But Guizot couldn't wait any longer, and the new Legion was shipped off to Algiers, under the command of a short, stocky ex-farmer from Brittany – *Chef de Bataillon* (Major) Antoine Bedeau, a brave and capable leader.

Under the hot African sun, the new recruits trained rigorously for battle. It was a tough and strenuous training, and only occasionally did a cool wind blow inland to refresh the men as they drilled and marched day after day, and practised rifle-shooting till they were crack marksmen.

By July, the Legion had grown to fifteen hundred

Below A Legion battalion drills on the parade ground in front of the fort. It was only by constant tough and strenuous training that the Legion could hope to survive in the desert.

Opposite A company of legionnaires march through the Sahara Desert. Many of the recruits had never seen such a barren landscape, nor lived in such a harsh climate.

men. This was enough to form an infantry regiment divided into two battalions. The system of national battalions introduced by Colonel Stoffel was abandoned. Bedeau wanted the different nationalities to learn to live together. Only in this way could a reliable, unified Legion be built up.

Once again, language barriers caused confusion. But the new Legion was not as large and unwieldy as the old one, and these problems were slowly overcome. Meanwhile the survivors of the old Legion struggled on in Spain for yet another year. After that, Bedeau's Legion became the only Legion.

The Maghreb

The Maghreb is the name given to a huge region of North-West Africa. Today it consists of three countries, Morocco, Algeria and Tunisia, but in 1830 it was made up of hundreds of small kingdoms. Each one was ruled by a bey, or, in the desert, by a sheikh. These kingdoms often fought between themselves, and were usually too weak and too divided to resist the powerful French army.

The Maghreb is split into three main regions. Along the Mediterranean Sea is a narrow coastal strip about fifty miles wide. It is here, where the

climate is good, that most of the people and wealth of the region are concentrated. And here the Arabs – a tall, dark-skinned race – lived in peace with the French invaders.

Behind the coastal strip lies the might Atlas mountain range. The bare rocky crags often rise to a height of three thousand feet, and are scarred by deep gorges. In the western Atlas, in Morocco, live the Riff tribes and, to the east in Algeria, are the Berbers. They are both tough warlike people, who differ from their northern Arab neighbours in language and customs.

South of the Atlas mountains lies the vast Sahara Desert – mile upon mile of sand, broken only by parched rocks. The temperature here can rise to 120°Farenheit at midday, and there is hardly any rain. The Sahara is inhabited by small tribes of Berbers called Tuaregs, who wear flowing black robes and ride tall, strong camels. The Tuaregs are nomads who wander from oasis to oasis, carrying their families and possessions with them.

When the French arrived in Africa, the coastal Arabs put up little resistance. But the Riffs, Berbers and Tuaregs refused to submit as easily, and France began a war which was to last for more than a hundred years. The tribes found it easy to ambush unsuspecting French patrols as they advanced slowly along the high mountain passes. And if the tribesmen were defeated in battle, they could take refuge in the labyrinth of mountain caves.

Abd-el-Kader was a Berber sheikh, and his strong leadership filled the inhabitants of the Maghreb with enthusiasm and hope. He swore that one day he would drive the hated French out of his land and straight into the Mediterranean Sea.

Regiments of the Legion

For many years, the Foreign Legion was only an infantry unit. In 1835, when the new Legion was formed, there were two battalions of about 750 men. By 1841, there were four battalions. These were divided into the First Foreign Regiment (*Régiment Etranger*) known as the First R.E. for short, and the Second R.E. Throughout the great desert campaigns, these were the only two regiments the Legion had. However, each R.E. was often made up of more than eight battalions – enough in normal circumstances to form six or seven full-sized regiments.

The French High Command would often ask one of the two regiments to send a detachment of legionnaires to attack a rebel Berber army, or to punish a Tuareg sheikh by raiding one of his desert oases. In such cases, the regimental commander would usually send two or three normal Legion battalions. But if it was an important mission, he would pick out a few hundred of his best officers and men, and form them into a special unit called a *Bataillon de Marche* (Shock Battalion). The tribesmen feared these special battalions most of all. They

knew that these legionnaires could march at a fast pace over long distances. They knew that they were acclimatized to the burning rays of the sun, and that they would not tire easily. And they knew that the battalion would never rest until it had found and defeated the tribesmen.

When the battalion had accomplished its mission, it returned to the Regiment, and the men went back to their normal duties. Much of the Legion's glorious battle record was won by these special units.

In 1918, the Third R.E. and Fourth R.E. were formed. Just before the outbreak of the Second World War, in 1938, they were joined by the Fifth and Sixth Regiments. And at the same time cavalry, tank and camel patrol units were organized. Finally, after the war, Paratrooper and Engineer Battalions were added to the Legion's strength.

The Legion was formed originally to complete the conquest of the African Maghreb and to make it a colony of France. It was while the Legion was still composed only of infantry that this task was accomplished.

Desert equipment

The French Foreign Legion was originally intended to operate only in North Africa, where the temperature can soar to over 100° Farenheit in the daytime, and drop to below zero during the long desert night. The colour of the landscape is mainly sandy brown. The Berbers and Tuaregs knew these conditions. They dressed in long robes of white or khaki during the day, and at night they wore black. The loose robes kept them cool in the sun, and could also be tied tightly around them for warmth when it grew cold.

The French High Command, in its plush Paris offices, never experienced the harsh conditions of the desert. For more than a hundred years Legion commanders begged for suitable desert clothing for their men, but without success. The sweltering legionnaires went on wearing the same infantry uniform as the French soldiers in the cold rainy regions of northern France.

The dress of the legionnaire changed little throughout the great desert campaigns. On his head he wore a blue kepi with a red top. A kepi was a round cloth hat with a leather peak. It gave him little protection against the sun. Later the legionnaire was allowed to cover it with a light khaki cloth which hung down at the back to protect his neck from the scorching rays. The sun soon bleached the khaki to a brilliant white, and to this day the legionnaires are still affectionately known as "the white-caps."

The main item of clothing was the heavy blue serge overcoat. It was useful to the legionnaire on sentry duty during the cold nights, but in the heat of the sun it became unbearably hot. After a long march

the coat would be damp with sweat and the blue dye would run, staining the man's shirt, trousers, hands and neck. The suffocating warmth made it hard to concentrate, but the legionnaire could not afford to overlook the hawk-eyed Tuareg snipers who might be watching him from afar.

The only sensible piece of clothing the legionnaire had were his heavy black leather marching boots. On his back he carried a cumbersome pack containing spare clothing, ammunition and rations. In his hand he grasped a long, accurate, Lebel rifle, and at his belt hung *Rosalie*, the long steel bayonet used in hand-to-hand fighting.

Above The clothing of the desert tribesmen had evolved through centuries of living in desert conditions, and was cool, loose and comfortable. In contrast, the uniform of the legionnaire (*right*) was quite unsuitable. It afforded little protection against the burning rays of the sun, and its dark colours provided an easy target against the sun-bleached landscape.

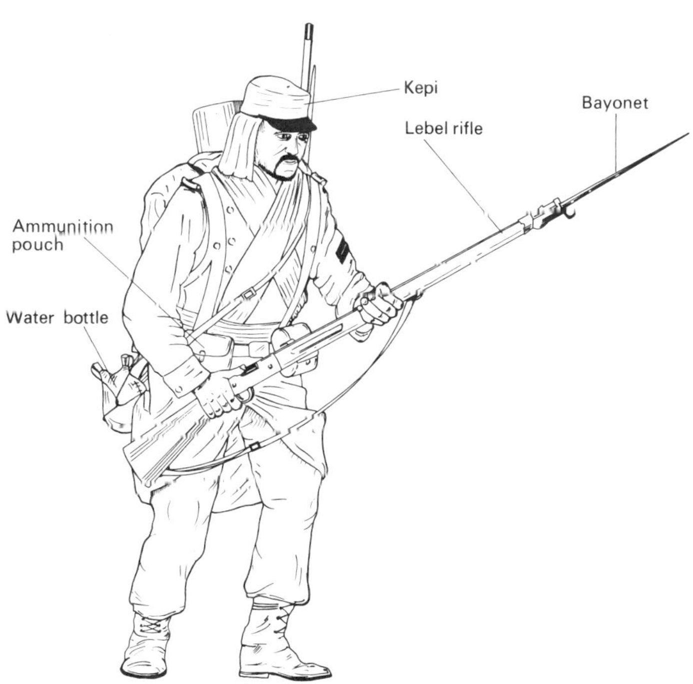

Conditions in the desert

Few of the men who volunteered for the Legion had ever set foot in Africa before. Some came from the cool countries of northern Europe, where sand was only found by the sea and rain was commonplace. Even the Italians, Spaniards and Greeks, who were used to a warm climate, were not prepared for their life in the barren Algerian desert.

The soldiers of the Legion were fighting two enemies – the Berber and Tuareg tribesmen on the one hand, and the desert on the other. Malaria, sunstroke and food poisoning were further hazards to be faced by the legionnaire.

Life in the Maghreb consisted of either garrison duty or campaigning. For months on end, a legionnaire might remain in his fort, many miles from the nearest town, waiting for an enemy attack or for orders to march. Time passed slowly for there was little to do in the fort. Most legionnaires spent their spare time in the café, drinking cheap Algerian wine and brandy. The bored soldiers were always getting drunk and fighting among themselves – it helped to pass the time.

Below Peeling potatoes for the evening meal. Garrison duty in the Legion was extremely monotonous and, in their boredom, many men started to drink the cheap Algerian wine, and to fight among themselves.

Eventually a battalion would receive the order to march. The constant ache of boredom was over for a while. But now a numb feeling of fear took its place. Campaigning meant days, sometimes weeks, of long hot marches – often thirty blistering miles a day. And the legionnaire never knew exactly where he was marching to. He carried enough water in his tin waterbottle to last for two days. After that he had to rely on his officer to find an oasis deserted by fleeing Tuaregs. But if the wily tribesmen had poisoned the water before leaving, then the legionnaire had to manage without. And even one day without water would swell his tongue, dry out his skin and weaken his will to march on.

Meanwhile, the legionnaire was constantly aware that the merciless tribesmen were watching his every movement, waiting for him to grow tired, looking for a chance for an ambush. If he fell wounded, or strayed from his companions, there was no hope for him. He would be tortured and killed by the tribesmen, or would die of sunstroke, alone in the desert.

Below The order to march came as a welcome relief to the legionnaires cooped up in their fort, even if it did mean the risk of attack and death from the fierce desert tribesmen.

Tactics against the tribesmen

In 1839, General René Bugeard took over from the ageing General Guizot as Commander-in-Chief of the French forces in the Maghreb. He was a tall artillery officer from Strasbourg, a town in eastern France, trusted both by his men and by his superior officers. It was this trust which brought him to the rank of general at a very early age. His face was thin, but his body was extremely powerful. Indeed, he was so well built that he never looked smart in his gold and blue uniform. The muscles bulged on his arms and shoulders, and his large hands hung awkwardly out of his sleeves.

When Bugeard arrived in Algeria in 1839, he found the French units there tired and demoralized; they longed for their new commander to lead them to final victory over the Berbers in the Atlas mountains and the Tuaregs in the Sahara desert. To do this Bugeard felt it necessary to introduce new methods of warfare, adapted to desert conditions. As an artillery officer he knew the value of a large cannon. Its explosive shells could be hurled two or three miles with uncanny accuracy. He also knew that the war in the desert was a fast moving war. Legionnaires sometimes had to march a hundred miles in a few days in order to catch an unsuspecting enemy at rest in a remote oasis.

So the General established the famous "flying columns." These detachments were usually made up of a *Bataillon de Marche*, strenghtened by two field cannons. The cannons were dismantled and carried

Above A Legion flying column, with the mules carrying artillery on their backs, struggles up the mountainside to attack a Berber camp.

on the backs of sturdy young mules who, for safety's sake, walked in the middle of the column. When the battalion was ready to attack, the cannons were reassembled and loaded, ready to fire.

Every good general likes to get things done with as little bloodshed as possible. So Bugeard let the tribesmen know that, if they behaved peacefully, the Legion would not disturb them. But if they attacked a fort, or raided homes built by French settlers, a flying column would be sent out against them. This scared the tribesmen. The great fire power of the cannons and the brutal determination of the legionnaire with his bayonet were an enemy to be feared. And they knew that the men of the flying columns would not give up until they had found the Arabs, and punished them.

A system of forts

The Sahara Desert is a vast area. The flying columns developed by General Bugeard were very effective, but they could not operate further than a hundred miles afield. Beyond that, they needed food, fresh mules and ammunition. So Bugeard began to set up desert supply dumps. These were built along the main desert routes, at intervals of about fifty miles. They usually consisted of a cluster of tents and were often sited near a water-hole. A small garrison of legionnaires and doctors guarded the supplies and assisted the flying columns on their arduous journeys.

The legionnaires nicknamed these dumps "biscuit-towns." This was because they always stocked huge stores of salted meat and the brown biscuits which were the basic field rations of the Legion. The biscuits were so hard that the men had to dip them in water or wine to make them soft enough to eat.

The tribesmen soon realized, however, that without the biscuit-towns the relentless flying columns

Opposite A fort built by the Foreign Legion looks grimly out over the surrounding countryside.

Below Diagram and sketch of a typical Legion fort. The flag flying over the main gate indicated that the Legion was in residence.

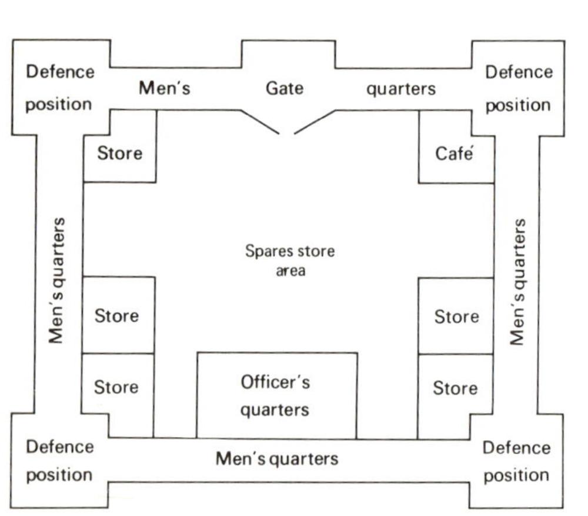

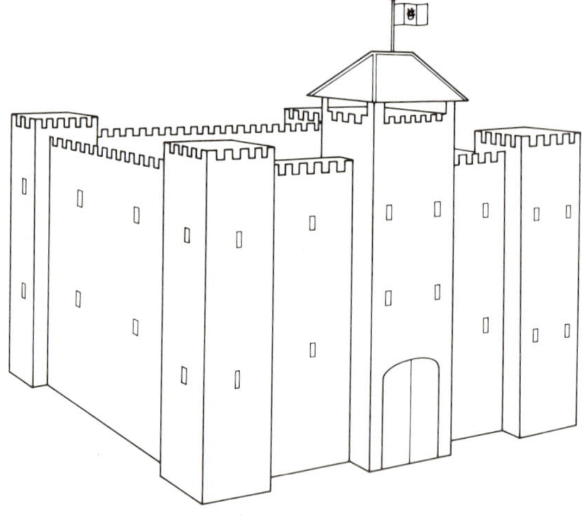

could not pursue them over long distances. So they made a series of surprise raids on the supply dumps. Many were burned to the ground, and their defenders slaughtered. These raids prompted General Bugeard to develop the sites into a system of forts, able to withstand prolonged attack. The first great fort was built in 1844, at Sidi-bel-Abbès, a small Berber oasis in the Atlas mountains. Gradually a large town grew up around its huge stone battlements. It contained the Legion's Headquarters, Museum and Archives, and became affectionately known as the "home of the Legion."

The forts further south in the Sahara were not as grand. They were usually square and built of wet sand baked hard by the sun. The outer wall and battlements were twenty feet high, and Legion sentries had to peer to see the ground below. There were no windows on the outside, and the legionnaires had to cut slits through which to fire their rifles. Within the walls were the living quarters, a hospital and a café. But the most important part of the fort was the supply area. Immense stocks of food and water, ammunition, rifles and cannons were the priceless treasures which the garrison guarded jealously, and were prepared to defend with their lives.

Tribal tactics

In 1831, a new Berber leader emerged to unite the Arab tribes against the French – Abd-el-Kader. Few Arabs on the coast believed that Abd-el-Kader was powerful enough to defeat the French. But the Berbers and Tuaregs had faith in him, and rushed to join his army. Soon he had eight thousand fully armed soldiers under his command, both cavalry and infantry. They armed themselves with home-made rifles, and with Lebels bought from Arab traders or stolen off the bodies of dead legionnaires. They brandished long knives with sharp, curved blades, whose thick handles were ornamented with precious stones and ivory.

The Berber cavalry were mounted on light brown Arab ponies – smaller than European horses, but very much faster. They could survive for days without water in the desert. The Tuaregs in the south rode tall, lumbering camels. By 1840, Abd-el-Kader had also captured some field guns which he now used in turn against the Legion supply dumps.

Abd-el-Kader's methods of attacking a flying column were consistent and effective. He would follow it at a safe distance until it was too far from a fort or supply dump to call for help, and then he waited for the hot desert sun to weaken the soldiers, and for the long march to make them tired and careless. When he judged that the time was right, his cavalry would appear from behind a sand dune or a rocky ridge. Waving swords and rifles they charged at the column at full gallop, racing to capture the mules before the legionnaires could assemble the cannons strapped to the animals' backs.

As the surprised soldiers rushed to find cover, the

Below A typical leader of a desert tribe. The tribesmen were skilful and wily fighters, and constantly harried the battalions of the Legion.

Below A column of Berber cavalry advances across the desert. Mounted on their hardy ponies, the tribesmen would follow a Legion detachment at a safe distance, and wait until the legionnaires were exhausted from thirst and the long march before attacking.

Berber horsemen retreated, if possible dragging the mules and the cannons after them. The foot soldiers then crept in, took aim with their rifles, and started to pick off the legionnaires one by one. Their colourful Legion uniform made them an easy target.

When the column had been annihilated, or the Berbers had grown tired of fighting, they would withdraw into the desert wastes as silently as they had come.

The campaigns in the desert

Abd-el-Kader was the greatest leader of the Maghreb tribes. He was young, determined, brave, and popular with his men. His aim was to capture Oran, an important port and one of the centres of French power in the 1830s.

Abd-el-Kader fought successfully against the French for many years. But General Bugeard sent wave after wave of flying columns against him, and the rebel Berber army was forced to retreat back into the Atlas Mountains in eastern Morocco. In December, 1847, Abd-el-Kader was captured at the head of a small, dispirited Berber detachment near Taza. These exhausted tribesmen were all that was left of the once proud army that had come so close to defeating the French.

By this time, Abd-el-Kader's bravery was legendary. The legionnaires treated him well in captivity. He was not killed, as so many prisoners were, but instead was sent to live in exile in Senegal – a French colony in West Africa. He died there in 1876, a tired broken man. But, even today, his name and the honour he won are remembered in the Maghreb.

No other leader came forward to take Abd-el-Kader's place and, for more than twenty years, there was an uneasy peace. Then, in 1870, his younger son, Abdelaziz Kaid, collected a Berber army of about ten thousand men from among the tribes of north-west Algeria. They caught the French by surprise, and burned two legion forts to the ground before flying columns were sent out to take revenge.

Kaid's success reawakened a fighting spirit amongst the Berber tribes near Constantine, in eastern Algeria. They rose in their thousands to attack the Legion again. But the revolts were not as serious as they had been under Abd-el-Kader, and the system of forts made resistance to the Legion at once more difficult and more risky for the Arabs.

After two years of combat the ferocious columns finally crushed the rebel forces. But complete peace never returned to the Maghreb. Abdelaziz Kaid continued to resist until 1908, when he was cut down by a Legion sniper. Other Berber leaders then took his place, and kept the torch of defiance burning from generation to generation.

Opposite Legionnaires fight their way up the barren hillside to attack a rebellious Berber village.

Below The main areas of North Africa in which the French Foreign Legion campaigned between 1830 and 1926.

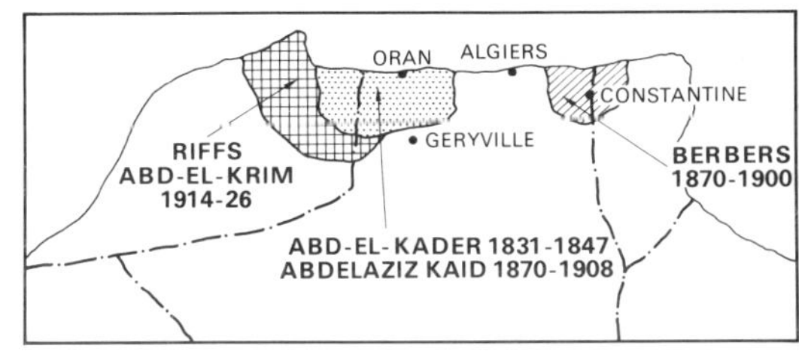

The Battle of Chott-Tigri

One of the Legion's most famous battles took place in 1882. The Ouled-sidi-Cheikh tribe of Berbers, under the leadership of Abdelaziz Kaid, had been terrorizing the mountainous region around Geryville – a small town of mud houses, dominated by a legion fort, in north-west Algeria.

The morning of 26th April dawned crisp and fresh. The flying column of legionnaires from the First R.E. marched smartly out of the fort. The column was made up of two infantry companies and one mounted company, with one mule for every two men.

As the column was passing through a deep gorge in the Atlas mountains, a sandstorm suddenly blew up. Blinding clouds of sand cut into the legionnaires' faces. They squinted through half-closed eyes, trying to keep each other in view. In the midst of the storm, a force of about 1,800 heavily armed Berber cavalry charged at the bewildered column.

The mounted company formed a rough square out of the bloodstained carcasses of mules shot by the Berbers. The rest of the column rushed through the blinding sand to take up battle positions in this makeshift fort. As they did so, Berber horsemen galloped among them, hacking at their fear-filled faces with long curved swords.

After half-an-hour, the surviving legionnaires had crowded into the square of mules. Their earlier panic now disappeared as they performed the drill movements they had rehearsed so often. They pointed their long Lebel rifles at the enemy, and directed volley after volley of murderously accurate rifle-fire at the cavalry and foot-soldiers who advanced warily towards them.

The battle raged throughout the day and the following night. Then, just before dawn, the Berbers suddenly vanished into the desert. The sandstorm had died down, and the exhausted legionnaires looked out on a scene of violent desolation. More than two thousand Berbers, out of an army of almost five thousand, were corpses in the sand. The column had lost seventy-four men out of the original three hundred.

As the legionnaires plodded wearily back to Geryville, they remembered the warnings of their older comrades. Life in the Legion was hard. But it was also full of glory.

Left The discipline of a few hundred legionnaires, in their serried ranks and squares, enabled them to repulse the attacks of five thousand Berber tribesmen at the famous battle of Chott-Tigri, in 1882.

Left Map showing the route followed by the French Foreign Legion Brigade on their way to fight in the Crimean War of 1854–56.

Opposite During the siege of Sebastopol, the legionnaires were forced to camp out in the frozen wastes of the Crimea. They had insufficient clothing, little food, and no fuel to keep them warm.

3. Some other campaigns

The North African desert was not the Legion's only battleground. The legionnaires were sent to fight, and to die, in any war which the High Command knew the French people would not support.

One such war was the Crimean War of 1854–56. France fought on the side of Britain and Turkey against the mighty armies of Russia. Each of the two Legion regiments was ordered to provide three *Bataillons de Marche,* and these were formed into the Foreign Brigade – totalling about five thousand men.

Misfortune haunted the Brigade from the start. The ship carrying the legionnaires to southern Russia sailed through the eastern Mediterranean and into the Black Sea. It stopped at the port of Varna, a small but important town on the coast of Bulgaria. There an epidemic of cholera had broken out, and many in the Brigade were struck down with it. When the ship finally reached Sebastopol, the capital city of the Crimean peninsula, five officers and two hundred men had already died of this horrible disease.

The Brigade immediately joined the French and British armies which were besieging Sebastopol. It was December, 1854, and one of the coldest winters Russia had ever known. The legionnaires were ordered to dig deep trenches in the frozen ground, there to take cover and wait for the order to attack. But the men had not been issued with proper winter clothing. Many of them suffered from severe frostbite as they lay shivering in the cold. Every week, cholera claimed more victims from among those in the dirty wooden huts which served as hospitals. Their tearful comrades looked on helplessly, for the disease was incurable in those days.

Finally, the storming of Sebastopol began. The legionnaires, weakened by cold, hunger and disease, attacked the fanatical Russian defenders as best they could. In September, 1855, after particularly savage fighting, the town was captured at last. As usual, the Legion had shown itself to be the bravest of all the units engaged in the bloody siege, but it had also lost the most men. When the Brigade was shipped back to Algeria in June, 1856, more than two thousand of its men were left behind, dead from the cold, wounds or cholera.

The glorious battle of Camerone

Above In Mexico, a small convoy of legionnaires, led by the gallant Captain Danjou, were ambushed by a large force of rebels outside the hamlet of Camerone. They fought bravely all day but, by nightfall, only three legionnaires remained alive.

Right A map of Mexico, as it was when the legionnaires went there in 1863.

The strangest war which the Legion ever fought was waged in Mexico, during the rule of the Emperor Maximilian. He was an inexperienced and rather rash young man, and Mexican rebels were quick to rise in revolt against him. As the Emperor was an ally of France, three battalions of the First R.E. were sent to Mexico City to help Maximilian in January, 1863. They joined a strong contingent of regular French troops who were already there fighting the rebels.

Before dawn on 30th April, 1863, a French convoy set out from the tiny town of Maledra, to march the two hundred miles to Mexico City. The soldiers packed bars of gold on the backs of their mules, to pay the loyalist Mexican troops. The convoy was accompanied by a unit of two officers and sixty-two legionnaires led by Captain Henri Danjou. He was

a brave officer, whose left hand had been chopped off by a Berber sword. In its place, he wore a false hand carved out of wood.

At 9 a.m., when the convoy was passing through the little Mexican village of Camerone, it was attacked by rebels. Colonel Milan, one of the rebel leaders, rode at the head of 800 cavalrymen and 1,200 infantrymen – all of whom were experienced soldiers.

With a wave of his wooden hand Captain Danjou gave the order: "Make for the white farmhouse!" Dragging the pack-mules loaded with the precious gold, the legionnaires rushed into a nearby farmhouse, which had been deserted by the local farmers. The battle which followed was both bloody and vicious. Both sides suffered heavy losses. Under the hot sun they grappled in grim combat as the Mexican rebels tried to capture the farmhouse.

By six o'clock in the evening, the sun was slowly sinking behind the purple mountains. Captain Danjou had been shot dead by a sniper several hours before. Lieutenant Maudet, a short stocky Parisian, was now in command. But there were only six men left to command. Everyone else was dead.

Maudet knew the battle was lost, but he also knew that a legionnaire must never surrender. He ordered his five men: "Fix bayonets! Charge!"

When the firing had stopped, only three legionnaires remained alive. They had tried to charge 1,700 Mexicans.

Indo-China

At the end of the nineteenth century the French, in their endless search for new colonies, turned their attention to the Far East. The first step towards conquest was made in November, 1883. A powerful force of soldiers, including a *Bataillon de Marche* of legionnaires, landed at the port of Haiphong, in the area we know as North Vietnam.

The French advanced gingerly along the left bank of the Claire River towards the important city of Hanoi. But their progress was blocked by the brick fort of Son-Tay. This fort was manned by two thousand Chinese soldiers known as "Black Flags." They were part of an army of 25,000 sent from southern China to stop the French advance.

The Chinese troops were armed with rifles, and with long spears which had curved, steel blades. Their leaders waved huge black silk flags to encourage the men in battle.

The French troops surrounded the lonely fort and, for two days, pounded it with cannon shells. But the black flags continued to wave defiantly in the breeze. There seemed to be no alternative – in order to continue their advance on Hanoi, the French would have to storm the fort.

The French commander, General Negrier, ordered the *Bataillon de Marche* to lead the attack. He then told his artillery to concentrate their fire on the wooden gates of the fort. After accurate shells had blasted a hole in them, the legionnaires charged, screaming war-cries as they pointed their bayonets at the Chinese. The first man through the shattered gates was a sergeant. His path was immediately blocked by a huge Black Flag soldier, who cut him

Opposite In order to make any headway in Indo-China, the French were forced to capture the fort of Son-Tay, which was strongly defended by a large garrison of Chinese soldiers. Here the Legion commanders discuss the best way of breaching the walls of the fort.

Below A map of Indo-China, showing the main areas where the French were involved in fighting.

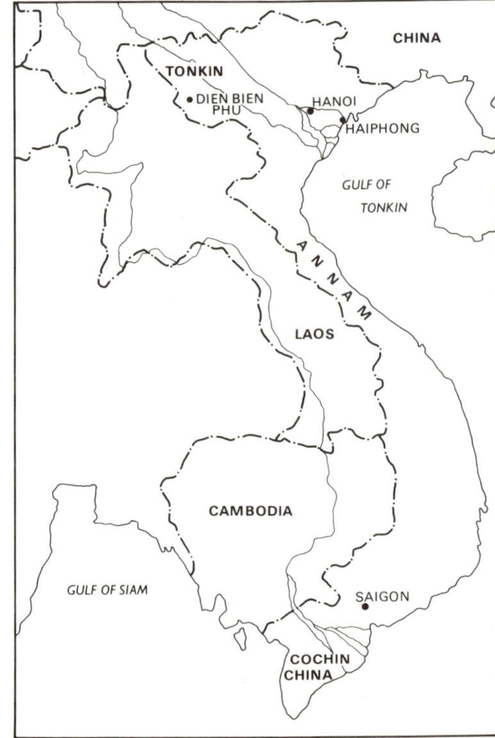

almost in two with a swift sweep of his spear. The other legionnaires stopped fearful in their tracks as the sergeant fell dead to the ground. But then a young officer jumped over his body, and shot the Chinese through the head with his revolver. This restored the men's courage. They charged on into the fort and, after two hours of bloody fighting, the black flags of the enemy were replaced by the red, white and blue Legion flag.

The Black Flag army fought on for two more years. When they surrendered, in 1885, the French had virtually completed the conquest of Indo-China.

4. Kurt Drecker

Kurt Drecker stared at the words on the poster. He could barely read French but he understood the phrase: *Engagez-vous à la Legion Etrangère*. The poster was pinned up on the sooty wall of a café in Paris. As the young German boy repeated the words to himself, he remembered the reasons that had brought him to the French capital in search of a new life.

Kurt was born on Christmas Day, 1874, in the small country village of Hermannstadt in western Germany, two miles from the French border. His parents were poor, and as soon as Kurt was six he had to go out and help them, and his two brothers and sister, to work the small farm which they owned. He milked the cows, guarded the pigs and fed the thin white chickens.

But Kurt was an intelligent boy. He wanted to see the world. He was not content to spend all his life struggling to make a living on the farm. As he led the cows to the fields each morning, he dreamed of distant places – of the mysterious lands of China and Japan, of the damp jungles of Africa and of the sweeping sand dunes of the Sahara Desert.

One cold February morning in 1890, Kurt's patience finally came to an end. He woke up early, dressed quietly in his warmest clothes, took the little money he had managed to save, and tiptoed out of the front door. Only when he had walked a good half-mile along the muddy road that led to France did he heave a nervous sigh of relief – at last he was really on his way. After walking for another hour, he saw a road sign in the darkness. It welcomed him to Aubesville, the first village over the French border.

It took Kurt four months to cover the three hundred miles to Paris. Most of the time he walked. Sometimes a passing horse and cart gave him a lift to the next village. Often he spent a few days at a farm doing odd jobs to earn enough money to buy food and continue his journey.

Kurt reached Paris on a hot sultry day in July. He had no clear plans. He did not even really know why he had come to Paris. But as he read the poster, he made up his mind. From now on, the Legion would be his life.

Opposite A romantic picture of Arab life, far removed from the brutal reality faced by the legionnaires. But it was probably just such a picture which fired Kurt's imagination, and encouraged him to seek his fortune in the French Foreign Legion.

A new recruit

Kurt walked around the dusty Paris streets for an hour or more before he found the Legion barracks. It was a cluster of square brick buildings five storeys high, surrounded by a grey stone wall. The gate was guarded by two muscular sentries, sweating in the thick blue overcoats and heavy leather equipment which they had to wear even in the hot July sun.

As Kurt walked timidly up to them, the taller of the two – a corporal – pointed his rifle at Kurt's chest and asked him what he wanted.

"I want to join the Legion," Kurt stammered.

A broad grin spread across the legionnaire's face. A man had to be eighteen before he could enlist. It was obvious that this boy was scarcely more than fifteen years old. But he put down his rifle and pointed to a small office just inside the main gate.

"That's where you join," he said.

Inside the office sat a fat, red-faced Adjutant, called Bussel, who announced that he came from Bavaria in southern Germany. Kurt was relieved to meet another German. He began to pour out the long story of how he had come to join the Legion. But Bussel quickly put a finger to his lips, motioning Kurt to stop talking. Then, in regulation French, he asked him the usual questions.

Firstly, what was Kurt's name? Kurt did not want to give his real name. He was afraid the friendly legionnaire would betray him and tell his father where he was. Bussel, noticing Kurt's hesitation, snapped that the Legion accepted a man under whatever name he decided to give. Then he asked Kurt's nationality, and if he was medically fit. Finally he asked his age. Kurt blushed. As he gritted

his teeth and said "Eighteen," it was obvious he was lying. Bussel stared at the boy, smiled quietly to himself, and wrote "Eighteen" on the recruiting form.

There were no more questions. The Adjutant told Kurt that he was now a soldier in the Foreign Legion. If he was wanted by the police for any reason the Legion would shield him. If he had joined up to find a new life, the Legion would make sure that his old life never caught up with him.

Legio Patria Nostra

On the first day of every month all the recruits accepted at the Paris barracks were sent to the Fort of Sidi-bel-Abbès, the headquarters of the Legion, for basic training. In July, Kurt was the only new recruit. And, on 1st August, he boarded the train to begin the long journey to North Africa, as so many legionnaires had done before him.

Kurt was accompanied by Sergeant José Delgados. José was a small bearded soldier from Malaga in southern Spain. His eyes were large, black and mournful. On the uncomfortable two-day journey to Marseilles, he hardly said a word to the nervous but excited German recruit. But, as their ship left the crowded harbour of Marseilles and set off across the Mediterranean to Algiers, José became more cheerful. He seemed to like Kurt, and told him many stories about the Legion.

José had joined in 1836 while the Legion was fighting the Carlists in Spain. Later, when the old Legion was disbanded by Louis-Philippe, José stowed away on a Spanish cargo boat bound for Algiers. There he soon enlisted in the new Legion which was being formed.

After twenty-four years of faithful service, José had only managed to reach the rank of Sergeant. But he was happy. The Legion was his whole life. Kurt was enthralled by every word the little legionnaire uttered. Finally, José explained to him the famous Legion motto – *Legio Patria Nostra* – "The Legion is our Homeland."

When a man joins the Legion, his nationality changes. He is no longer an Englishman, a Russian or an Italian. He is a Foreign Legionnaire. If he has a passport, it is taken from him. He belongs to the Legion now. He must go where it sends him, and obey its orders without question. If he tries to

desert, the Legion pursues him. If he is recaptured, he is punished severely. But if the Legion is hard, it is also kind. It takes the place of a man's family. It pays him, feeds him and protects him. If he gets drunk and is arrested by the police, the Legion secures his release and punishes the legionnaire in its own way.

As José smiled, Kurt realized that the little Spaniard had found a homeland in the Legion. He loved it more than anything else in the world.

Above These legionnaires have abandoned all ties with home and country. From now on, the Legion is their homeland.

Opposite The famous flag of the French Foreign Legion. The colours ran from left to right, blue, white and red, with a yellow grenade on the centre panel. The number of the unit was printed inside it.

Basic training

As Kurt and José approached the huge fort of Sidi-bel-Abbès, the Spaniard's attitude suddenly changed. They were still comrades, but from now on José was the sergeant, and Kurt the raw untrained recruit.

They went straight to the office of the Commandant, Colonel Jean Perenne. He was a hard master. Legionnaires trained by him endured six weeks of back-breaking work. But the lessons he

taught later saved their lives in skirmishes with the wily Berber tribesmen.

Kurt joined about fifty other recruits. They were all billeted in the Recruits' Barrack Room. That first afternoon Kurt lay on his hard bed with its prickly straw mattress, and looked at his new comrades. There were men of fifty, and boys scarcely older than he was. There were flat faced Russians, burly Germans, chattering Italians and gloomy Norwegians. But all were united by the motto, *Legio Patria Nostra.*

At four-thirty the next morning, a fat, bad-tempered Sergeant-Major, called Kowolski, kicked open the door of the dormitory. He walked down the long room roughly pulling each man from his bed. As Kurt crashed onto the hard concrete floor, he woke with a gasp of pain. Outside, the desert night was still bitterly cold. Even before he was fully awake Kurt was pulling on his stiff white trousers and buttoning his thick blue overcoat. As he bent over to lace up his boots, Kowolski lifted him by the belt and carried him bodily outside. Then he threw him onto the sand, baked solid by the sun and hardened by the stamping boots of countless soldiers.

The next six weeks seemed an eternity. Kurt was drilled from early morning until seven o'clock at night. He marched fifteen miles a day, and practised rifle-shooting and bayonet charges for hours on end. He polished his equipment until it shone. And he suffered Kowolski's continuous brutality.

But soon he felt his muscles swell and harden. He was growing stronger. It was a proud day when, in September, he and the other recruits paraded before Colonel Perenne. Each one was handed the coveted white cap-cover and neck-shield. They were real legionnaires at last.

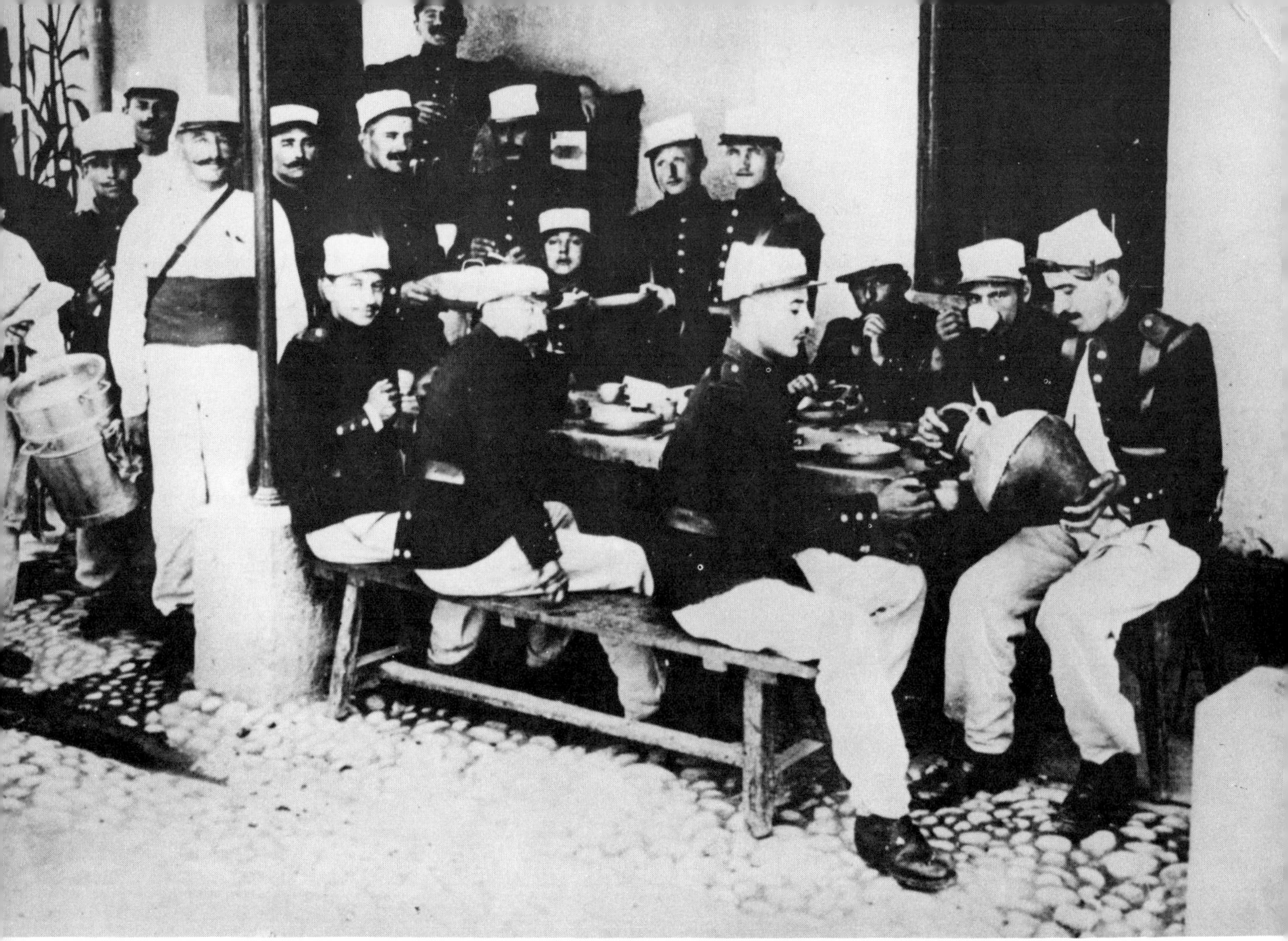

A way of life

Once the shock of the training course was over, Kurt's life settled down to an unchanging routine. He was still woken up at four-thirty in the morning, but the sergeants were no longer as brutal. Kurt's white kepi had made him one of them. After jumping out of bed, he quickly dressed. Then he shaved and washed in the huge barrel of cold water which had been placed outside the door of the hut the night before. By morning it was usually almost freezing.

Above Legionnaires pose for a photograph while eating their main meal in the shade of the terrace. They were usually served soup, salted meat, rice, potatoes and beans, with rough Algerian wine to wash it down.

At five o'clock Kurt had breakfast. It was always the same: the famous dry Legion biscuits, some salted beef or pork, and hot black coffee. At six o'clock, the working day began. He carried out his duties until eleven. By this time the sun had climbed high in the sky. The air had grown dry and hot, and the wind had dropped. The temperature was about 95° Fahrenheit. Everyone stopped work for the morning.

From then until four in the afternoon, the soldiers lay on their beds, or sat lazily in the cafés of Sidi-bel-Abbès drinking wine or brandy. It was too hot even to move. The dazzling reflection of the sun from the white walls of the buildings hurt Kurt's eyes. He was off duty now. He could walk around in trousers and shirt, but the white cotton stuck to his sweating body.

Between four and seven the men worked again. Then they had their second meal of the day. This was the main meal, and it was a big occasion. They were served soup, more salted meat, rice, bread, potatoes, and long green beans. The men ate together on long wooden tables in the canteen. At one end, slightly apart, sat the officers. They were waited on by some of the local Berbers, who were paid a few francs a day to do odd jobs around the fort. After the meal Kurt was free. The Legion did not care what he did or where he went, as long as he was ready for work again at six o'clock the next morning.

The days were monotonous. Kurt soon became bored. This was not the life of adventure he had expected. He knew most of the other soldiers felt the same way, but they seemed to be resigned to it. Indeed, they appeared to take pleasure in complaining about their life. The grumbling helped to keep them sane.

Tasks and duties

After a few months at Sidi-bel-Abbès, Kurt realized that a legionnaire's life is a mixture of great danger, extreme boredom and hard work.

Road building had become a Legion tradition since Colonel Stoffel and his men had built a large part of the coast road eastward from Algiers. While Kurt was at Sidi-bel-Abbès, the Legion was building a road to the oasis of Saidi, nearly fifty miles away to the south. Every morning, at six o'clock, Kurt and a squad of soldiers marched twenty miles to the head of the road and began the day's work.

First, they had to smooth out the roadway with heavy steel spades. Then they put down gravel, which they flattened into the ground with their stamping boots. It was back-breaking work. If Sergeant-Major Kowolski was on duty he made the legionnaires work through the midday rest period, while he lay in the shade of a large blue and white umbrella. Kurt began to hate Kowolski.

At least once a week Kurt and the men of his company had to do a thirty-mile route march. For two hours before the march, the men cleaned all their equipment. Kurt washed his trousers and cap-cover till they were sparkling white. He polished his boots, leather belt and cartridge cases. Then he dismantled his precious Lebel rifle, cleaned and oiled the parts, and put it together again. Finally he polished *Rosalie,* his bayonet, and even the spare bullets he carried in his belt-cases.

The march was long. The men had to carry full battle equipment, including the thick blue overcoat. They marched for an hour and then had five minutes rest. This punishing pace lasted all day. A legionnaire had to learn to march without food or shade – to prepare for the day when his life would depend on it.

By the time they got back to the barracks, the men were covered from head to foot with a thick layer of dark brown dust. Sweat had stained their trousers, and made their overcoats damp. But, before they were allowed to eat a well-deserved meal, they had to clean their clothes and equipment until they were as smart as when they had left the fort that morning.

Below Men of the Foreign Legion at work building a road in Algeria. Road construction was a traditional Legion task, but for the new recruits it was back-breaking work.

Recreation

At first Legionnaire Kurt Drecker had no real free time. As soon as the midday rest period came, he stumbled wearily to his bunk and collapsed onto the hard bed fully clothed. There he slept soundly until a bugle-call sounded the return to work. He staggered back into the sunshine, counting the hours before he could return to bed.

But, as the months went by, Kurt's body grew stronger, and he became more used to the work. He made friends with a talkative young Frenchman called Jacques Leclos, who had joined the Legion by pretending to be a Belgian – normally Frenchmen were forbidden to serve as legionnaires.

One day Jacques suggested that they should go into the native quarter for a drink and a game of cards. Kurt agreed eagerly. The two soldiers chatted happily as they walked together along the dark streets of Sidi-bel-Abbès. They wore their white kepis, white shirts and white trousers with blue sashes around their waists. They were easily recognizable as legionnaires. Jacques knew a bar on the edge of town where the Berbers sold good, cheap, red wine. They entered the low gloomy building, which was lit by two smoky oil lamps. A fat Berber, with a long black beard and a thick curved dagger tucked in his belt, recognized Jacques and invited them both to play cards.

The evening wore on. Kurt and Jacques became more and more drunk. Finally, Jacques's head crashed onto the table, and he began to snore loudly. Kurt was barely awake himself, but he could see the Berber stealthily reach out his hand to pull the wallet from his friend's hip-pocket. In a flash the Frenchman stood up and was wrestling furiously with the native. Other Berbers came forward. Then Jacques, seeing he was outnumbered, shouted at the

top of his voice the famous cry for help . . . *A moi, la Légion* – "To me, the Legion."

Within seconds, ten burly legionnaires had burst through the flimsy wooden door and attacked the surprised Berbers with their fists. In five minutes, it was all over. An hour later Kurt woke up. He was lying on the earthern floor. The bar was empty except for the body of his friend. Jacques lay slumped over the card table, the Berber's dagger sticking from his back.

Desert madness

Perhaps it was his friend's death that caused Kurt to be struck down with *le cafard*, "the desert madness." Perhaps he would have suffered from it anyway. Life in the Legion had driven many an experienced soldier to the edge of lunacy, and Kurt was barely eighteen.

When Kurt had recovered from the first shock of the murder, he determined to find the fat Berber who had killed Jacques. Every night he wandered the dark narrow streets looking for him. In his relentless search he visited every bar he could find. The more he looked the more he drank the cheap red wine. But he could not find the murderer.

Kurt's nerve finally snapped one day when he was on road-building duty. Kowolski was in charge, and the sadistic Pole was in a bad mood. He sat watching as Kurt and the others, stripped to the waist, dug their heavy steel shovels into the rocky desert ground.

Kurt was still half-drunk from the night before. The sun beat down on his head. His kepi did not seem to protect him at all. He felt weak and helpless. His body was numb with the work and the wine. Then Kowolski shouted at Kurt. Dimly, the young German heard the words: "Work harder!"

Kurt stared at the Pole. In his half-crazed brain, Kowolski's face seemed to change, until before him stood the Berber he had sought for so long.

Kurt ran up to Kowolski and his hands, bruised and blistered by the spade, fastened around the Pole's throat and clawed at his windpipe. But Kowolski was too quick for him. His solid fist crashed into Kurt's jaw and the young legionnaire fell unconscious to the ground.

When Kurt awoke he was lying in a clean soft bed in the Fort's hospital. At the head of the bed hung a grubby white card with *Le Cafard* scrawled across it in sooty black ink. The doctor, a kindly old Commandant, stood by him. He told Kurt that he had been delirious for six days. But the worst of the desert madness was over.

Kurt never suffered from *le cafard* after that. He realized that, in order to survive, he had to harden his mind just as he had been forced by the Legion to harden his body.

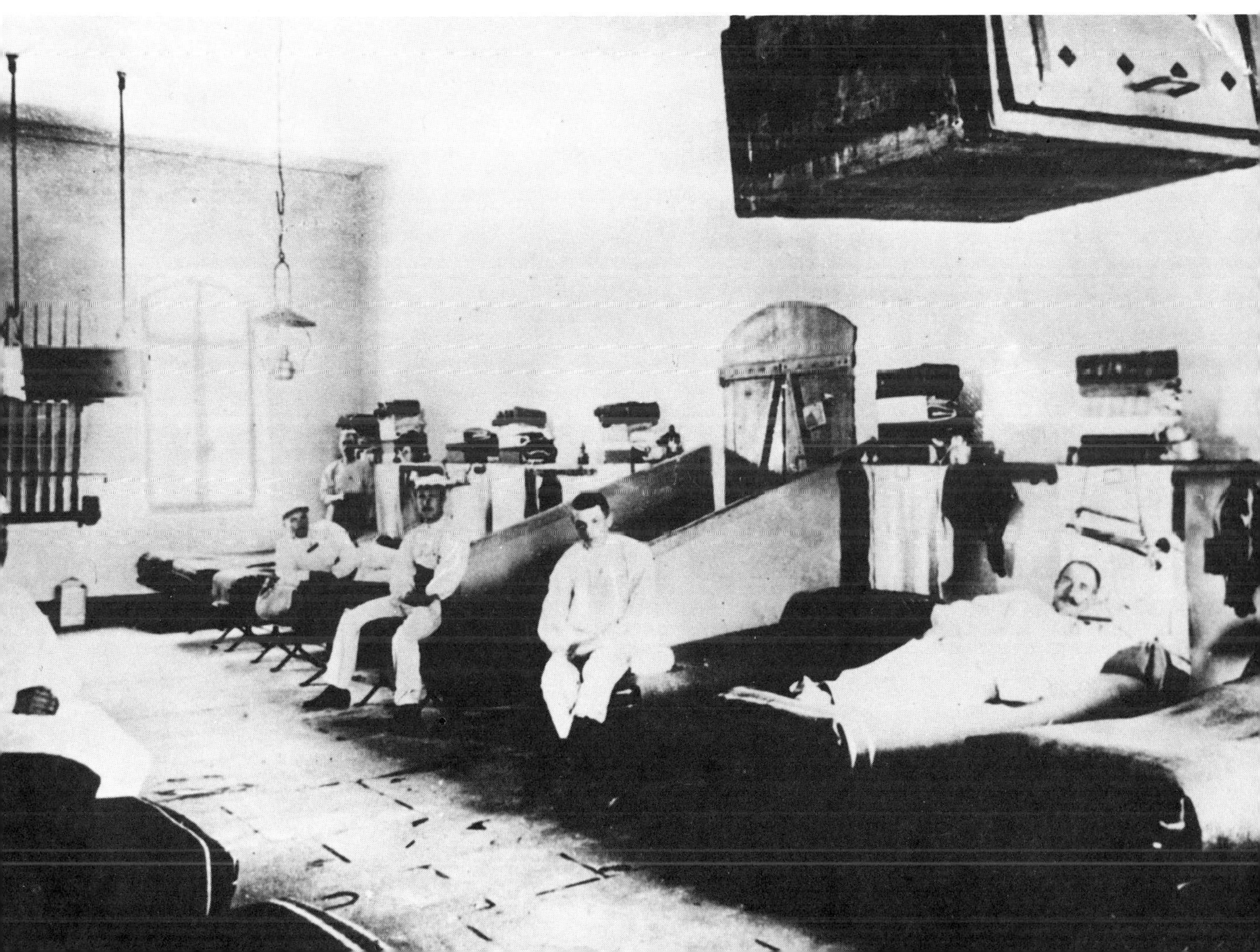

Brutality

Kurt went back to the Second Company after two weeks in hospital. For the next month he did not see Kowolski. A tribe of Berbers had attacked a supply dump at Tlemcen, an oasis about sixty miles from Sidi-bel-Abbès, and Kowolski was ordered to join a *Bataillon de Marche* which had been hurriedly formed from the more experienced troops at the Fort.

Kurt secretly hoped that the fat Pole would be killed by a Berber dagger, just as his friend Jacques had been. But exactly thirty days after he had left, Kowolski marched proudly back at the head of the battered flying column. The story he told was a grim one. The column had been ambushed in a deep mountain pass. The battalion's four officers had been killed. Kowolski had taken command, fought bravely, and put the tribesmen to flight.

Kowolski returned with as great a hatred for Kurt as Kurt had for him. The Pole took every opportunity to make life unbearable for the young German. It was quite normal in the Legion for sergeants to hit the men under their command. Many of the legionnaires were criminals who had joined the Legion to escape from the police. The officers believed that violence was the only way to make them obey orders. Even so, Kowolski deliberately picked on Kurt. If it was his duty to wake the men in the morning, he rushed straight to Kurt's bed, lifted the sleeping soldier off the mattress, and threw him brutally onto the hard concrete floor.

The other legionnaires watched this treatment helplessly. They could do nothing. Kowolski was a sadist. And Kurt could only suffer and hope that the Pole would grow tired of his brutality. It was strictly forbidden for a soldier to strike a sergeant-major. And Kurt's friends warned him not to complain to the officers about Kowolski. The officers respected

the Pole. He was a brave fighter and a good leader. And he could make the men work hard. If Kurt did complain to them, Kowolski would call Kurt a liar and the officers would believe him. Then they would leave him to deal with Kurt in any way he liked. Anyway, to complain about another legionnaire was disloyalty – and this was a great crime in the Foreign Legion.

Desertion

During those miserable days Kurt seriously thought of deserting from the Legion. The older legionnaires had often talked to him about desertion, so he knew how to set about it.

The rate of desertion has always been high in the Legion. Many men joined for adventure, or to escape from their past life. But they did not realize that they were joining the toughest unit in the French army. Many found that the life they had left behind was easy compared with the life they were now enduring. Out of the Legion garrison of three thousand, about thirty deserted every month.

Above A steamer unloading at Oran, one of the main ports of Algeria. Oran was a favourite escape route for deserters from the Legion, but it was heavily patrolled by the Legion's military police, the *Gendarmerie Etrangère*.

Kurt knew the escape routes. Most deserters made their way northward to the port of Oran, where they could usually find a ship returning to Europe. But this route was dangerous. The Legion hates deserters. It tries hard to recapture them. So the main ports, especially Oran, were heavily patrolled by the Legion's Military Police, the *Gendarmerie Étrangère*. These men had an uncanny sixth sense for spotting deserters. It was usually safer to travel west, to Tangier in Morocco, and then to cross into Spain.

Because there were so many deserters, groups of unscrupulous Arabs and Europeans, often ex-legionnaires themselves, set up escape organizations. Every legionnaire knew the name of one such man living near the fort. For a sum of French francs, he hid the deserter in his home until the gendarmes gave up their search. Then he took him to a port and smuggled him aboard a boat which would carry him back to Europe.

If a deserter was caught by the Legion, he was immediately court martialled. If he was a corporal or a sergeant, he lost his stripes and the extra pay that went with them. He was reduced to the lowest rank – Private Second Class. He was then sentenced to a term in the notorious Legion Prison at Sidi-bel-Abbès.

But the Legion prides itself to this day on being a volunteer force. It does not want to keep soldiers against their will. When a deserter has completed his prison sentence, which is usually between six months and a year, he is given a choice. Either he can leave the Legion legally, or he can start again as a private, with a clean record.

Promotion

When Kurt had finished his recruit's training at Sidi-bel-Abbès, he was given the lowest rank in the Legion – Private Second Class. In most armies he could have become a corporal within five years. But the High Command does not like foreigners to gain high ranks in the Legion. Kurt remembered Sergeant José Delgados. It had taken him twenty years to reach his rank.

But if rank stripes were hard to win, they were even harder to keep. José Delgados had been demoted to private several times. One day he had got drunk in town. He accidentally upset a café table and broke some plates and glasses. Almost at once he was seized by two gendarmes and marched back to the fort. There the gold sergeant's stripes were torn from his sleeves.

But José was not worried. The Legion needed good sergeants. After about a month he would be given back his rank. But, meanwhile, the other sergeants could make life difficult for him. This would also teach him not to be too brutal when he became a sergeant once again. While he was a private, the

other legionnaires would be able to pay him back
with their fists for any time he had treated them
unfairly. The exception was Sergeant-Major
Kowolski. The Pole took good care never to lose his
rank. He knew that there were too many legionnaires, Kurt included, who would love the chance to
lay a hand on him.

After twenty years' service in the Legion, a
legionnaire could become a citizen of France. He
would be given a French passport and could return
to France to live when he was discharged from the
Legion. Or he could stay on and try to become an
officer. Every officer in the Legion must be of French
nationality. But it does not matter whether he was
born in France, or became a French citizen later.
Once he is an officer, a man can rise to high ranks in
the French army, and can also transfer to the regular
cavalry or infantry.

Up to now, no legionnaire who was not born a
Frenchman has ever reached the rank of general.
The High Command respect the Legion as the best
unit in the Army. But they have never forgotten
that the Legion was recruited from the unwanted
and homeless soldiers of Europe.

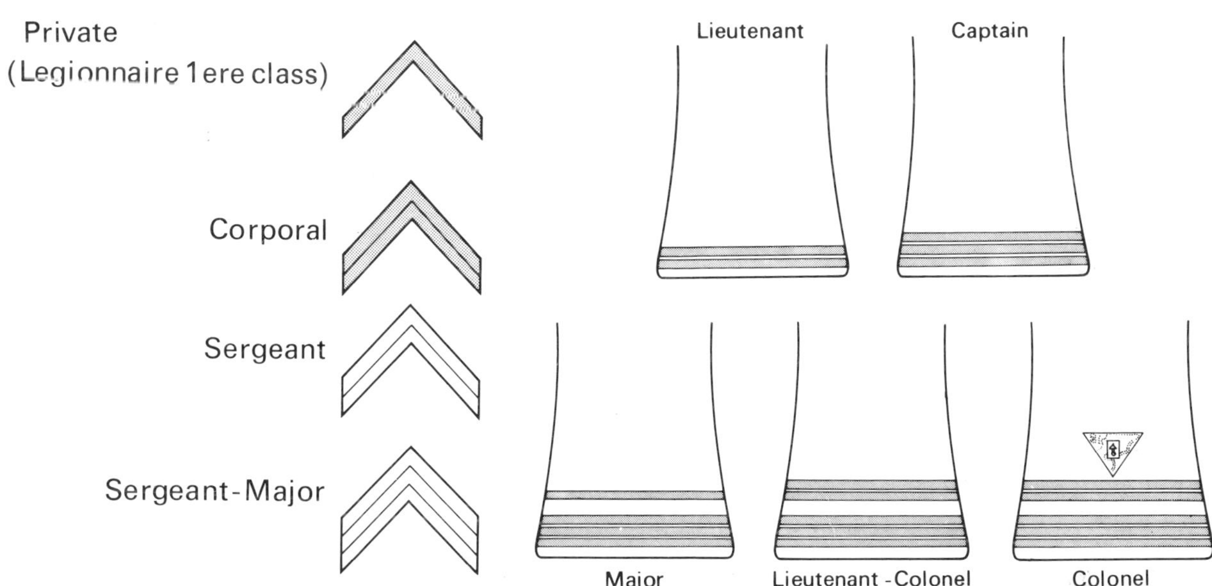

Shaped by the Legion

Kurt Drecker joined the Legion in 1890. Twenty-nine years later, as a man of forty-five, he retired from service. He had reached the rank of Adjutant, or Warrant Officer. The Legion gave him a bounty in gratitude for his service. Kurt had often dreamed of all he would do when he left the Legion. But, on this his last day, his eyes were wet with tears.

Colonel Georges Caret, the commander of the First R.E. in which Kurt had served, shook his hand warmly at the farewell parade. The whole regiment were lined up in their best uniforms. The white kepis, the well brushed blue overcoats, the sparkling white trousers, and the shining equipment all reminded Kurt of the hard years he had spent as a legionnaire.

Kurt wondered what he would do now. The Legion had been his whole life. He had joined it when he was still a boy. He could never return to his father's farm in Hermannstadt. He had not heard from his family since he had joined the Legion. They probably thought he was dead. He had no wife or children. The Legion had been his family. He had often cursed it and wanted to desert from it, but now there was nowhere else to go. He was too old to change.

At last Kurt did what so many legionnaires had done before him. He used the bounty to buy a café in Sidi-bel-Abbès. He had been popular in the Legion, and soon had a thriving business. The officers and men, when they were off duty, would drop in to see him and have a drink. As he served them the sweet black coffee, or red wine, he could see the tall gateway of the fort where the Legion's flag still hung limp at the flagpost.

Kurt wondered if the Legion had changed him.

It had helped him to grow up. It had made him hard. If anyone, legionnaire or Berber, caused trouble in the café, Kurt was quick to throw them out. It had made him self-reliant. Even when things were going badly he always felt the inner strength to carry on. The Legion had given him confidence in his own capabilities.

The Legion above all had been a friend, a family and a homeland to Kurt. He knew that he could never live far from those tough men in their white kepis.

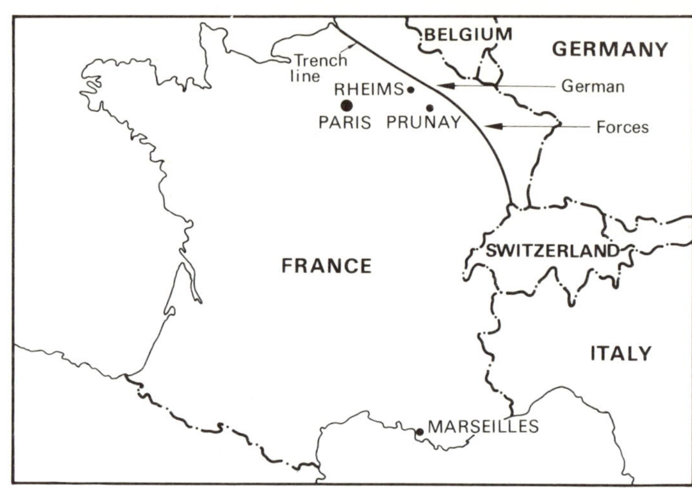

5. Later campaigns

In August, 1914, France and Britain declared war on Germany and Austria. Almost immediately a strong German army advanced through Belgium towards Paris. The French High Command was panic-stricken. Its Commander, General Joffre, mobilized the huge French army. He also called upon each of the two Legion regiments still stationed in Algeria to send a *Bataillon de Marche* to help fight the Germans.

The Legion Commander was Colonel François Périgot, who had spent his whole military career in the Legion. He picked the best officers, sergeants and legionnaires that he had. In September, 1914, the two battalions left Algiers for Marseilles. They arrived on French soil to find that the German army had almost reached Paris. In this grave emergency, the High Command called upon young Frenchmen to volunteer for the Legion. Within a month, six battalions had been formed from these raw but enthusiastic recruits. They joined the two regular battalions to form the *Brigade Etrangère*.

Meanwhile, the French and German armies had both come to a halt. They faced each other along

a line of trenches, reinforced with wooden planks, which stretched from the Swiss frontier to the Channel coast. In October, the Legion Brigade was sent to reinforce this line near Prunay, a town near Rheims in eastern France.

At first the old legionnaires, fresh from desert skirmishes, despised the young volunteers. But, as they faced death together in the damp, open trenches, all bitterness disappeared. They spent day after day waiting for the German soldiers to attack from their trenches, which were half a mile away. Sometimes the legionnaires would be ordered to advance and attack. They crept out of their earthen holes, trying to duck below the German machine-gun fire. Few of them got as far as the enemy trenches. Their losses were so great that their officers quickly ordered them back to their own lines. There they cowered. They had lost hundreds of men and gained no ground.

When the two armies eventually ceased fighting in 1918, the survivors of the Brigade returned to Algeria bitterly disappointed. They had achieved so little in the muddy warfare of the trenches.

War against the Riff

When the weary and disheartened Legion Brigade returned to the Maghreb in 1919, it was reformed into two new regiments – the Third and Fourth *Régiments Etrangers d'Infanterie*. They were badly needed, for new trouble was brewing in North Africa. The Riff tribesmen of northern Morocco had watched the Brigade leave for Europe in 1914. They then proceeded to attack the weakened Legion garrisons.

The Riffs were commanded by a new leader, Abd-el-Krim. As a boy, he had been sent to school in

Opposite A blockhouse used by the Riff tribesmen in their campaign against the French in the Maghreb. The Riffs led by Abd-el-Krim were the first tribesmen to use modern European fighting methods.

Europe, and when he returned to the Maghreb his ambition was to free it from the hated French. But he intended to use European methods to do so.

Abd-el-Krim's army was more than ten thousand strong. He had cavalry armed with swords and rifles, and foot soldiers who carried rifles and daggers. He had also brought from Europe some field cannons and three fighter aircraft. The simple tribesmen were not skilled enough to operate this modern equipment. So the cunning sheikh had built up a force of two hundred Europeans, mostly deserters from the Legion. He paid them well to serve him as mercenaries. These men did not hesitate to help their old enemy, and to kill the very legionnaires who had once been their friends.

Abd-el-Krim organized savage attacks on the Legion forts. By the time the Legion Brigades returned to provide reinforcements, nine forts had been burned to the ground, and the outnumbered legionnaires had been forced to abandon thirty others. But when the Legion was once again at full strength the tide turned against the Riffs. Fighting was fierce as the flying columns marched off into the Atlas mountains of Morocco. Each legionnaire was careful to keep a spare bullet in his pocket. If he was in danger of being captured, it was better to shoot himself than to die in agony at the hands of the merciless tribesmen.

It took the Legion seven years to bring the war to an end. Finally in May, 1926, Abd-el-Krim was taken prisoner in his mountain hide-out. The Legion's punishment was swift. He was executed on the spot by a firing squad. Once more an uneasy peace descended on the Maghreb.

Cavalry and armoured cars

By the end of the First World War, life was beginning to change for the Foreign Legion. Since 1830, it had been an infantry force, trained to fight and survive in the desert, with only wits, bravery and rifles for support. But war was becoming a more complicated business. An army made up only of foot soldiers was no longer viable.

In 1921, the French High Command decided to introduce a cavalry unit into the Legion – the First

Below Cavalry units of the French Foreign Legion march proudly past during a parade in Algiers. After the First World War, cavalry began to play an increasingly important role in the Legion.

Régiment Etranger de Cavalerie, or First R.E.C. for short. The men were mostly recruited from among Russian soldiers, who had fled their country when the Communists took control in 1917. They were experienced cavalrymen with no homeland, and it was hardly surprising, therefore, that they turned to the Legion for a new life. The cavalry were mounted on the same small brown horses that Abd-el-Krim's famous horsemen were riding. This was the time when the war against the Riffs was at its height, and the Legion cavalry did valuable work tracking the wily tribesmen through the mountains. Moreover, they gave the flying columns the extra speed and striking power that they desperately needed.

In 1939, a second regiment was formed – the Second R.E.C. But the men of the new regiment did not ride horses. Instead, they drove the new Panhard armoured car. The horse was out of date in a modern army. And the proud Russians of the First R.E.C. were told by the High Command that from now on they too must drive armoured cars.

Some Legion cavalrymen refused to do this. They deserted rather than give up their beloved horses. Others tried to explain to the High Command that a horse was essential in the desert. It was true that it was not as fast as an armoured car when travelling on flat hard ground, but much of the Maghreb is rocky soil or soft sinking sand. The wheels of an armoured car could plunge deep into the sand. A horse's hooves, on the other hand, prevented it from sinking. A horse needed only water to survive in the desert. An armoured car needed petrol, oil and spare parts.

But these protests were in vain. The Legion lost a faithful ally in the horse, and a short but glorious chapter of its history was closed for ever.

Above Two French soldiers in London salute the emblem of the Free French army (October, 1941).

Tragedy in Syria

The Second World War lasted from 1939 to 1945. In May, 1940, the French High Command sent three *Bataillons de Marche* to assist the Norwegians, who were fighting the powerful German army of Adolf Hitler. These Legion forces were called the Thirteenth *Demi-Brigade de la Légion Etrangère*, or Thirteenth D.B.L.E.

The legionnaires fought bravely in the deep snows of Norway. But, slowly, they were forced to retreat towards the coast. Finally they were taken by ship from the port of Narvik to England. There they joined other French troops which had been evacuated from France, and together formed the Free French army, under the command of General Charles de Gaulle.

In June, 1940, German tanks entered Paris. The French army was defeated. Marshal Philippe Pétain took over the government and promised to live in peace with the German conquerors. All French army units, including the Legion regiments still stationed in the Maghreb, received orders to stop fighting the Germans and to cease helping the British.

Only General de Gaulle in England disobeyed Pétain's command. In June, 1941, he sent two battalions of the Thirteenth D.B.L.E. to the Middle East, to help British troops conquer Syria. Syria was a French colony, but still under the control of Pétain, who had sent the Sixth R.E.I. there from Algeria to resist the invasion.

As the British and Free French troops advanced towards the desert capital of Damascus, the Sixth Regiment was sent to the surrounding hills to ambush them. The fighting was terrible. Desperately the infantrymen of the Sixth Regiment attacked the tanks of the Thirteenth Brigade. As they clashed in furious combat, many a legionnaire must have recognized an old friend on the other side. The losses were great. But all the legionnaires felt it was their duty to fight the enemy with all their might, no matter who they were.

When the clouds of sand cleared, the men of the Sixth lay dead around the Thirteenth's armoured cars. The victors cared for the enemy wounded, but nothing could heal the great wound that they all felt. It was a terrible tragedy that two units of the Foreign Legion had been forced to make war on each other.

Below King George VI is accompanied by General de Gaulle (on the right of the picture) when he reviews men of the French Foreign Legion during a visit to the Free French forces in Britain (1940).

War in Indo-China

In 1947, the first Legion units were sent to Vietnam, which then was part of the French colony of Indo-China. Vietnamese forces, under the famous General Giap, were fighting to make their country independent from French rule.

It was a bloody war during which many lives were to be lost. And it was typical of the French High Command that they should choose to send the

Legion to that distant Asian country.

As the war dragged on the Legion was joined by other French forces. The Vietnamese did not fight during the daytime. Legion patrols spent weary days marching through the sticky jungle without even seeing an enemy soldier. At night they returned to their forts to rest. It was then that Giap's forces attacked.

The Vietnamese moved up quietly and surrounded the fort. Suddenly a Legion sentry noticed the shadowy figures and called the alarm. The exhausted legionnaires dragged themselves from their beds to defend the fort. They battled bravely with rifles and bayonets, but the Vietnamese only attacked when they knew there were at least two of them to every one defender. After a few hours the fort was captured, and then it was burned to the ground.

The war lasted seven long years. It ended at the village of Dien-Bien-Phu, in North Vietnam, in April, 1954 (see map page 42). The French forces in that area, including some legionnaires, were surrounded by a huge army of Vietnamese. Giap ordered his gunners to destroy the village with their cannon. And the French troops cowered helplessly, in trenches and concrete bunkers, as thousands of shells exploded among them.

Finally most of the village was captured by Vietnamese assault troops. All that was left was the small Headquarters hut, defended by fifty survivors of the Third R.E.I. Deliberately, the Legion officer ordered his men to fix their bayonets to their rifles. They were going to charge the enemy, just as Captain Danjou's men had done at Camerone in 1863. With a great shout the legionnaires commenced their charge. They had run about fifty yards before they were all killed by machine-gun fire.

Algeria

In 1956, Morocco and Tunisia were promised full independence from France. But the French government had no intention of letting Algeria go, and the people of Algeria decided to fight for their freedom, just as the Vietnamese had done so successfully. The Berber and Tuareg tribesmen were at last joined by the Arabs of the Mediterranean coast, and together they formed a modern army which was determined to get rid of the hated French.

In 1955, the First and Second *Régiments Etrangers Parachutistes*, or R.E.P.s, were formed from Legion volunteers. These men were the pick of the Legion – tough, battle-hardened veterans who would fight to the death. The parachutists did not wear the traditional white kepi. Instead, they wore a green beret with a silver badge showing an eagle's wing and a sword.

These regiments joined the other Legion forces in their struggle against the rebels. They were used to fighting in the open desert and mountains, but most of the war took place in the coastal towns where the Arabs had the advantage. They could easily ambush unsuspecting soldiers in the dark alleyways, and then quickly escape.

In 1958, General de Gaulle was President of France. As it gradually became clear that the war in Algeria could not be won, he promised that the rebels would be given independence in 1961. The legionnaires were horrified. They had fought for more than a hundred years to keep Algeria French. They could not forget all the sacrifices they had made. Many legionnaires, particularly in the First

Above The distinctive badge worn on their berets by members of the Legion's two parachute regiments.

Opposite French Foreign Legion soldiers march out of the great fort at Sidi-bel-Abbès, the home of the Legion for so many years.

R.E.P., refused to obey de Gaulle, and they joined other French soldiers to form a rebel French army.

This revolt was soon crushed, however, and the Algerians received their independence as the General had promised them. And all the French soldiers, including the Legion, had to leave the country.

The legionnaires were heartbroken as they marched out of the great fort of Sidi-bel-Abbès for the last time. Algeria was lost and the Legion was in disgrace for its part in the rebellion against de Gaulle. The First R.E.P. was disbanded. It seemed to be a matter of only a few weeks before the rest of the Legion would share its fate.

6. The Legion today

France has changed considerably since those dark days of 1961. The vast barren deserts of the Maghreb and the Sahara, which used to form French North Africa, are now divided among half-a-dozen independent states. There is no longer a permanent base for the Legion on the continent of Africa, for these new states have no intention of allowing French troops to operate there.

The only colonies which France still owns are scattered all over the world. None of them are very large. But if France can survive without its

Below The Legion today is a force of technical soldiers, specialists in the art of war. Here a group of legionnaires use amphibious vehicles in the marshes of Vietnam.

vast colonies, it cannot do without the Foreign Legion. The Legion's reputation for bravery has grown steadily ever since its formation 140 years ago. It is now acknowledged as the best unit in the French army. So, even when Algeria was lost, the government could not bear to disband the Legion. A new job had to be found for it.

A new job was found. The French Foreign Legion is today an élite corps of about 14,000 men, enough for six regiments. It is no longer a unit of infantry, trained to march, fight and survive in the harsh Sahara Desert and the barren Atlas mountains.   It has become a force of technical soldiers – specialists in the art of war.

Each legionnaire is picked to do a specific task. If he is an infantryman, he now learns to fight from helicopters or armoured cars. These vehicles speed him right to the heart of enemy forces. He can then deliver a surprise attack and withdraw as quickly as he came.

The legionnaire might be a paratrooper. Or he might train as a frogman, learning how to swim into enemy harbours, plant deadly limpet mines on the hulls of destroyers, aircraft carriers and transport ships, and then escape silently through the water. It is strange to see legionnaires dressed in white ski clothes and wearing skis and snow shoes. Although they are the descendants of desert soldiers, they have now been trained to fight in snow or extreme cold.

The Foreign Legion has become a kind of emergency police force. Whenever the High Command needs soldiers who have nerve as well as technical skills, it knows it can rely on the Legion.

Life in the modern Legion

If Kurt Drecker were alive today, he would hardly recognize the modern Legion. He had spent his career in the Algerian desert, based most of the time at Sidi-bel-Abbès, the "Home of the Legion." In those days the legionnaire was the soldier nobody wanted. The French High Command wanted to conquer and keep the Maghreb. And if that meant the deaths of a few soldiers, then it was a price worth paying. The life of the legionnaire in North Africa was a mixture of boredom, fear and danger. He was bullied and punched by his sergeant, roasted alive by the cruel desert sun, and in constant danger of having his throat cut by stealthy Berber marauders.

That old life has gone for good. The Headquarters of the Legion is now at Marseilles, in southern France. This colourful seaport, the second largest city in France, was the place from which generations of legionnaires set off for Africa and a new life. Now it is the new home of the Legion.

The legionnaire of today has to be intelligent. He must learn to operate sophisticated new equipment such as helicopters, radio and radar. His weapons have changed. He no longer carries a Lebel rifle. He now has an A.A.52 machine pistol. This gun, made of stainless steel and painted a dull black, can fire sixty bullets a minute with deadly accuracy. It is only issued to the best French troops. He learns to fire bazookas, whose shells can pierce the armour of a tank. He operates missile launchers, which can send a rocket from the ground to destroy low flying aircraft.

The legionnaire lost *Rosalie*, the bayonet which had served him so well, during the Second World

War. He is now trained to use a double-bladed commando knife. He creeps silently through the night, grabs the unsuspecting enemy sentry by the neck and stabs him.

The Legion today treats its men well. There are no more cruel desert marches. Helicopters carry them over long distances. Sergeants are no longer

sadistic bullies. They must earn the men's respect before they can lead them. Officers no longer have to be bribed to join the Legion. Indeed, every young cadet in the French army hopes to be posted to the Legion when he becomes an officer. There he will be the envy of his friends.

A modern uniform

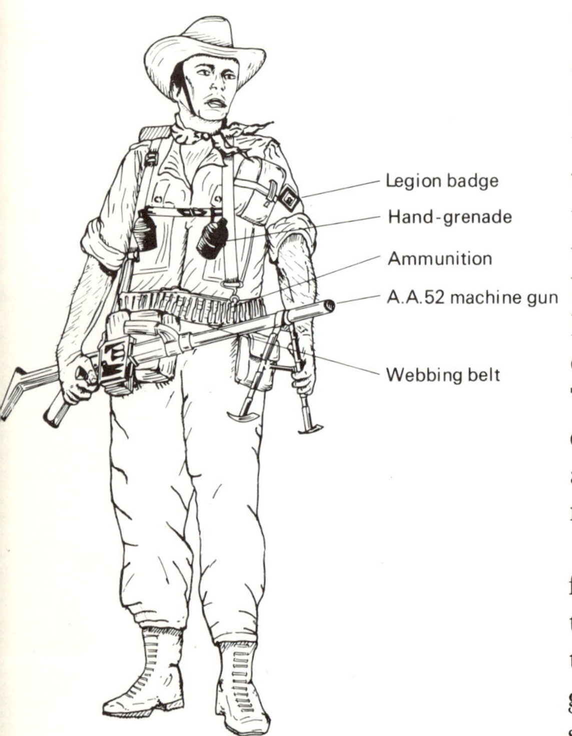

Above A modern legionnaire in battle dress. The uniforms of today are a lot more practical, if less colourful, than the uniforms of old.

Today armies are using more and more complicated equipment, but their uniforms are becoming simpler and less colourful. Kurt Drecker had only two weapons – his rifle and his bayonet. But his uniform was a sight worth seeing. He wore the famous kepi with the white cover and neck-guard. His overcoat was dark blue with gold buttons and red rank badges. His belts, boots and back-pack were of shiny leather. His trousers were starched and bleached a dazzling white. His waist sash was a deep royal blue. These bright colours stood out clearly against the drab desert background and made the legionnaire an easy target for the enemy. But he felt proud to march and fight in such a fine uniform.

Today, ideas have changed. A legionnaire must fight in a uniform which blends with the colour of the countryside. The best camouflage colour for both the Asian jungles and the European terrain is olive green. So he wears a shirt and trousers made of smooth green denim. They are loose fitting and comfortable.

He wears no medals or regimental badges when fighting. If he is captured by the enemy, they will not know which unit he belongs to. He is only allowed to wear small green stripes if he is a corporal, or gold ones if he is a sergeant or an officer, and a small blue cloth diamond with the green Legion grenade badge on it. He wears dull green webbing belts on which he hangs hand grenades and the heavy clips of ammunition which he feeds into his A.A.52 machine pistol.

When the legionnaire is training in barracks or is off duty, he wears a different uniform. It consists

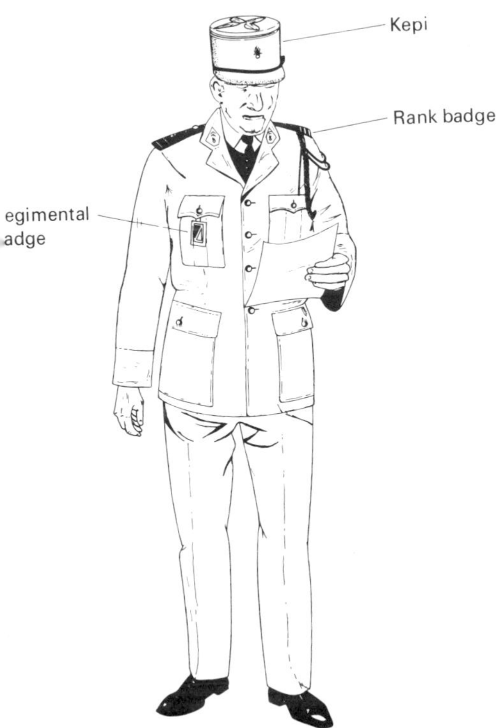

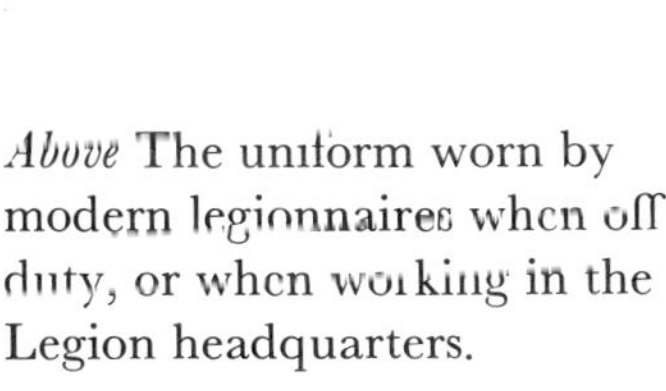

Above The uniform worn by modern legionnaires when off duty, or when working in the Legion headquarters.

Above right A modern legionnaire (on the right of the picture) stands in desert in his loose-fitting and comfortable uniform.

of a jacket and trousers of a rich khaki colour. On the jacket are his regimental badges, medals, and rank badges. On his head he wears the traditional white kepi, but in the cooler climate of Marseilles there is no longer any need for the white cloth neck-guard.

The legionnaire wears this drab uniform proudly, for it still represents the Foreign Legion. The small unit badges on his chest tell a long and glorious story. They are all that is left of the brave Legion regiments and battalions which fought so courageously to conquer North Africa for France.

The legionnaire of today

It is 30th April. This day is known throughout the Legion as "Camerone Day." The headquarters of the First R.E. is in the small industrial town of Aubagne, ten miles north of Marseilles. On this warm spring day, the whole regiment is on parade. The soldiers are wearing their best cotton khaki uniforms. Their medals and brass regimental badges sparkle in the bright Mediterranean sun.

The Adjutant calls them to attention – the Commander of the Regiment is about to speak: "You are the men of the Legion's First Regiment. You are a part of a great tradition which goes back over 140 years to the days of King Louis-Philippe. A legionnaire must always fight bravely. He must never surrender. When he has no more bullets left in his gun, he must attack with his bayonet or his bare hands, just as past legionnaires did at Camerone and Dien-Bien-Phu. If he is wounded, he must continue to advance, even if he has to crawl."

When the short traditional speech is over, the oldest sergeant in the regiment marches past the men. On his left is an officer carrying the red, white and blue flag of the French Republic. On his right another officer proudly holds the Legion's flag. The sergeant himself carried a glass box. In this, on green velvet, lies the wooden hand of Captain Danjou, who led the heroic defence of Camerone on 30th April, 1863.

The legionnaire does not forget the past. But he is also a part of the modern world. Frenchmen can now enlist as ordinary legionnaires – but any man, whether French or foreign, must prove that he is

Above Although the legionnaire now has machines to help him, he must still be physically very tough, able to withstand great extremes of temperature, able to fight with little food and little protection in barren and dangerous countryside

more than an average soldier and is worthy to wear the Legion uniform. There are fewer deserters. A man must be very sure of himself before he is allowed to join such a select group.

The training period now lasts four months. It is tougher than anything Kurt Drecker ever knew. The legionnaire must still be physically strong. He must be able to fight in intense desert heat, or in the bitter Arctic cold. He must be able to fight without much food or protection against the weather. But he must also be able to think for himself, and to use complicated weapons. He is part of a proud tradition of great men who went before him, and gave the Legion the enviable reputation it enjoys today.

The future of the Legion

The Legion has passed through, and survived, many bad periods. For years, the French High Command plotted deviously to get rid of the troublesome foreigners. Finally they realized that this strange group of homeless soldiers was the finest military force France possessed. Now jobs have been found for it all over the world.

The Legion's regiments are serving France well. The First R.E. is at present training recruits in France. The Third R.E. is based in Madagascar, a large tropical island off the east coast of Africa. It is helping the Madagascan government to keep the rebellious jungle tribes under control. Tahiti is a small island in the Pacific ocean with tall palm trees and soft white sands. It is a colony of France, and is used as a base for French scientists to carry out astronomical research and to follow the progress of French satellites. The Fifth R.E. is stationed there. It is carrying on the Legion tradition of road building and construction work.

The Thirteenth D.B.L.E., the heroes of the Free French forces during the Second World War, are guarding one of France's last colonies in Africa – the tiny region of French Somaliland in the north-east of the continent. The Second R.E.P. is the only Legion unit involved in a war at the present time. It is helping the government of the African state of Chad in the south of the Sahara Desert. There Tuareg tribesmen have rebelled against the government, which is controlled by Africans. The legionnaires, trained in desert warfare, are doing an excellent job.

As long as armies exist, France will need the skills of the legionnaire.

Opposite An officer of the French Foreign Legion commands native troops in Chad during their struggle against rebel insurgents. This is just one of the places in the world at the moment where the French Foreign Legion are engaged in keeping the peace.

Table of dates

<table>
<tr><td>1830</td><td>Louis-Philippe becomes King of France and disbands all foreign regiments in the French army.
Algiers is captured by the French, and the conquest of the Maghreb begins.</td></tr>
<tr><td>1831</td><td>Colonel Stoffel recruits men for the Foreign Legion in Paris. The Algerian sheikh, Abd-el-Kader, leads a revolt against the French.</td></tr>
<tr><td>1835</td><td>Legion forces distinguish themselves at the battles of Moulay Ishmael and Macta.</td></tr>
<tr><td>1835</td><td>The Legion is sent to fight the Carlist army in Spain.</td></tr>
<tr><td>1836</td><td>A new Legion is formed to fight in Algeria.</td></tr>
<tr><td>1837</td><td>The new Legion, led by Bedeau, arrives in Algeria and begins to train for action.
The old Legion suffers a heavy defeat in Spain at the Battle of Aragona.</td></tr>
<tr><td>1838</td><td>The old Legion in Spain is disbanded.</td></tr>
<tr><td>1839</td><td>General René Bugeard succeeds General Guizot as Commander-in-Chief of the French forces in the Maghreb.</td></tr>
<tr><td>1844</td><td>The great fort at Sidi-bel-Abbès is built by the legionnaires.</td></tr>
<tr><td>1847</td><td>The rebel leader Abd-el-Kader is captured and sent into exile in Senegal.</td></tr>
<tr><td>1854</td><td>The Foreign Brigade sails to the Crimea.</td></tr>
<tr><td>1854–55</td><td>French and British troops lay siege to Sebastopol, the capital of the Crimea.</td></tr>
<tr><td>1863</td><td>Captain Danjou's unit is massacred in Mexico at the famous Battle of Camerone.</td></tr>
<tr><td>1870</td><td>Abdelaziz Kaid leads a Berber revolt against the French in Algeria.</td></tr>
<tr><td>1876</td><td>Death of Abd-el-Kader in exile.</td></tr>
<tr><td>1882</td><td>Legionnaires win a glorious victory over the Berbers at Chott-Tigri.</td></tr>
<tr><td>1883</td><td>A Legion battalion sails to Indo-China to help French forces fight the Chinese.</td></tr>
</table>

1885   The conquest of Indo-China is completed by the French.

1908   Death of the Berber leader Abdelaziz Kaid.

1914   Abd-el-Krim and the Riffs rise in revolt against the French in Morocco.

1914–18   The First World War. Legionnaires fight in the trenches of Europe.

1921   First Legion Cavalry Regiment is formed.

1926   The Riff revolt is finally crushed.

1939   The Second World War breaks out in Europe.

1940   Legion forces are defeated by the Germans in Norway, and so travel across to England.

France is conquered by the Germans. Marshal Pétain agrees to co-operate with Hitler.

General de Gaulle forms the Free French Army in England.

1941   Free French legionnaires clash with legionnaires loyal to Pétain in Syria.

1945   End of the Second World War.

1947   Legion units sail to Indo-China to fight the Vietnamese rebels.

1954   The French army is defeated by the Vietnamese at Dien-Bien-Phu.

Algerian rebels rise in revolt against the French.

1955   Two Legion Parachute regiments are formed.

1956   Morocco and Tunisia become independent states.

1958   General de Gaulle is made President of France, and promises Algeria independence.

French Army units in Algeria, including the First R.E.P., rebel against de Gaulle.

1961   The First R.E.P. is disbanded, and Legion units leave the Maghreb. The French Foreign Legion is re-organized.

1969   The Second R.E.P. is sent to fight in Chad, in central Africa.

Glossary

ADJUTANT The highest rank of non-commissioned officer. It usually takes twenty years for an ordinary soldier to reach this position in the French army.

ARAB A native of North Africa or the Middle East.

BATALLION DE MARCHE A shock battalion, a special unit made up the most experienced legionnaires, which was sent into the desert to track down Arab troublemakers.

BATTALION An army unit of between five hundred and eight hundred soldiers.

BERBER An inhabitant of the Atlas Mountains of Algeria.

BEY Turkish word used to describe the ruler or governor of a town.

BISCUIT-TOWN Slang term for the supply dumps used by Legion flying columns. They were later converted into forts.

CAFARD A form of madness common among Legion soldiers, which was induced by the harsh conditions of the desert, and the monotony of Legion life.

CORPORAL A low grade of non-commissioned officer. He can command a squad of four or five men.

COURT MARTIAL Court which tries people who are accused of offences against military law, such as desertion.

FLYING COLUMN A Legion detachment made up of a *batallion de marche* strengthened by two field cannons.

FOREIGN BRIGADE A unit of two or three Legion battalions sent to fight away from North Africa.

FOREIGN MILITARY POLICE Legionnaires selected to keep order in the Legion.

KEPI A round, cloth cap with a leather peak, traditionally worn by legionnaires. It was covered with a khaki cloth which hung down at the back to protect the neck.

LEBEL The standard rifle used by the Foreign Legion from about 1860 to 1920.

LIEUTENANT A junior officer, who normally commands a group of thirty men.

MAGHREB A large area of North-West Africa. Today it is divided between the countries of Morocco, Algeria and Tunisia.

MERCENARY A hired soldier, one who fights for money, especially in the service of a foreign power.

OASIS Fertile area in the middle of the desert.

REGIMENT A large unit in the army made up of about four battalions, or two to three thousand men.

REGIMENT ETRANGER The official title for a regiment in the Legion. Also called R.E. for short.

REGIMENT ETRANGER DE CAVALERIE The official title for the two cavalry regiments in the Legion. Also called R.E.C. for short.

REGIMENT ETRANGER PARACHUTISTE The official title for the two parachute regiments in the Legion. Also called R.E.P. for short.

RIFF An inhabitant of the Atlas Mountains in Morocco.

ROSALIE A Legion nickname for the long steel bayonet which used to be carried as standard equipment by all legionnaires.

SHEIKH The leader of an Arab tribe.

TUAREG An inhabitant of the Sahara Desert.

Further Reading

W. Blassinghame, *All about the Foreign Legion*, (W. H. Allen, 1960).

A. D. Hart, *Strange Company – The French Foreign Legion in Indo-China*, (Cassell, 1953) – the experiences of the legionnaires fighting Vietnamese rebels from 1947 to 1953.

C. Mercer, *The Foreign Legion*, (Barker, 1964) – an "eye-witness" account by one of the few Englishmen who joined the Legion.

E. O'Ballance, *The Story of the French Foreign Legion*, (Faber, 1961) – contains many interesting stories about life in the desert.

P. Turnbull, *The French Foreign Legion*, (Heinemann, 1964) – a detailed history of the Legion, from its foundation to the present day.

M. Windrow, *French Foreign Legion*, (Osprey Books, Men-at-Arms Series, 1971) – a short history of the Legion, including eight pages of coloured drawings of Legion uniforms from 1830 to 1970.

P. C. Wren, *Beau Geste* (John Murray, 1924) – an adventure story set in the desert, written by a former legionnaire.

Index

Picture Credits

The Publishers wish to thank the following for their kind permission to reproduce copyright illustrations on the pages mentioned: Radio Times Hulton Picture Library, *jacket* (back), *frontispiece*, 9, 10, 12–13, 16, 18, 20, 22, 23, 24–25, 26, 27, 31, 32, 33, 39, 40, 43, 44, 47, 48–49, 50, 52, 55, 57, 59, 60–61, 62, 64, 65, 66, 69, 70, 72–73, 74; the Mansell Collection, 14, 29, 34, 36–37; Associated Press Ltd., 19, 75, 76, 79, 80, 83, 85; Camera Press, 87, 89; Establissement Cinématographique et Photographique des Armées, *jacket* (front and flaps).

The maps and drawings were done by Gordon Associates Ltd.

Y
355
Th

Thomas, N.
THE FRENCH FOREIGN LEGION

DATE DUE

18055